Table of Contents

List of Figures

List of Tables

I.   Introduction

Background and Purpose

Mentoring is not specific to any one group of individuals, specific workforce, race, or advanced society. Over the past few decades, there has been a tremendous surge in interest and research in the area of mentoring (Allen, Eby, O'Brien, & Lentz, 2008). It is a benefit that anyone can take advantage of with the right dynamic relationship, culture, and environment. Mentoring serves to advance knowledge and experience from a mentor to protégé. Defined by the name, mentors have knowledge to diffuse to a less-knowing or experienced individual or individuals. This truth is commonplace because intelligence and wisdom tend to grow over time due to a wide range of experiences and other life enriching stimuli. The act of imparting experiences and stimuli advance the knowledge of willing protégés.

Mentorships help willing protégés develop a sense of professional identity and personal competence (Allen, Eby, & Lentz, 2006). Across areas of research, scholars agree that mentoring can be associated with a wide range of positive outcomes for protégés (Eby, Allen, Evans, Thomas, & DuBois, 2008). Research highlights the positive outcomes for the protégé. According to Allen et al. (2008), when measuring the mentoring experience, those that have mentors compared to those without can receive positive career-related and psychosocial support. As an area of scientific inquiry, workplace mentoring is a relatively new focus (Allen et al., 2008), and this pervasiveness more prevalently illustrates itself in the in the lack of studies associated with the USAF. Thus infrequently studied, mentoring is a fragmented concept in the USAF.

The dynamics of each mentor-protégé relationship may vary with the people, environment, and other stimuli involved, but there are common threads amongst them. For instance, studies have shown formal mentoring is better than no mentoring, but not nearly as effective as informal mentoring (Allen, 2006). Mentoring relationships can be both positive and negative, and this perception of the process can drive individuals from future relationships. For this reason, career-influencing factors have to be looked at more closely.

When anchored by overall stress, retention (turn over intent), job satisfaction, and organizational commitment, it is essential to discuss the positive and negative perceptions of mentoring on twenty-first century Airman. In this study, the focus is on mentoring and non-mentoring that occurs within the professional context of the USAF supervisor and subordinate relationship, and their perceived notions associated with overall stress, retention, job satisfaction, and organizational commitment.

Problem

On 1 November 1996, the USAF formalized Air Force Policy Directive (AFPD) 36-34 illustrating senior USAF leadership's dedication and resolve for the mentoring of Airmen. F. Whitten Peters, the Secretary of the Air Force, in 1996, intended for all supervisors to take on the role of mentor in order to enact cultural change in the USAF (HQ USAF/DPDE, 2000). This decree attempted to create cultural change intending to empower officers, NCOs, and civilian supervisors to pass on the principles, traditions, shared values, and lessons of the American Airman profession of arms (HQ USAF/DPDE, 2000).

Some Airmen have formal mentors, while others have unofficially attached themselves to knowledgeable leaders (informal). Moreover, another group of Airmen believes they have never

2

had a mentor or a need for one. Despite the fact that experts agree mentoring can be associated with a wide range of positive outcomes for protégés and mentors (Eby et al., 2008). This imparting of guidance based on life or previous work experiences may go unrecognized as mentorship due to the timing or method in which presented. AFPD 36-34 (2000) designates Air Force supervisors as mentors for Airmen in their chain of command. Despite being mandated, mentoring relationships enforcement in the USAF is not taking place. In fact, many Airmen have chosen not to have a mentor to assist them in navigating the turbulent waters of the USAF.

Personal observations have shown that mentoring relationships amongst active duty USAF members significantly influences perceived notions of overall personal stress, retention (turn over intent), job satisfaction, and organizational commitment. In civilian organizations, research efforts pertaining to this matter illustrate that mentoring is associated with positive outcomes for protégés in career related and psychosocial mentoring (Lentz & Allen, 2009). As well, research has indicated employees who receive mentoring experience added promotions, have higher incomes overall, and are more satisfied with respective pay and benefits (Ensure & Murphy, 1997). Non-mentored Airmen do not know what they are missing because they have never had a mentor while in the capacity of the USAF.

Summary

Informal and formal mentor-protégé relationships are prevalent both in the context of the commercial industry and USAF. In 1996, the Secretary of the Air Force mandated all officers, NCOs, and civilians supervisors execute the role of being a mentor. Yet still today not every Airmen believes he has a mentor. Airmen have proven themselves successful and rank progression resilient, but may have missed a golden opportunity to advance their knowledge amongst other advantages. This study utilizes data derived from the November 2008 Status of Forces Survey of Active Duty Members (USAF members n = 2487; mentored n = 1745; non-mentored n = 742) and a test of means to ascertain whether perceived notions of overall personal stress, retention, job satisfaction, and organizational commitment are higher when comparing mentored and non-mentored Airmen.

II.   Literature Review

Preface

Throughout history, mentors have been asked to perform functions and activities for the greater good or advancement of kings and other influential leaders, nation-states, and societies to name a few. The modern world is no different. Research shows that mentoring is associated with positive outcomes for protégé due to two primary functions provided by the mentor: career related advancement (i.e. sponsorship, exposure, coaching, protection, etc.) and psychosocial mentoring (i.e. role modeling, acceptance, and friendship) (Lentz & Allen, 2009). Generally speaking, successfulness in any profession whether military or commercial sector, directly correlates with mentoring relationships.

Mentoring is a developmental technique that precedes the waxing and waning of man's most influential ancient civilizations. The first recorded history of mentorship dates back to approximately 800 BC when King Odysseus' of Ithaca, entrusted his kingdom, household, and education of his son, Telemachus, to a trusted friend and companion (Carruthers, 1992). Aptly named "Mentor," this friend and companion performed a role and developed a title that has stood the test of time. In Odysseus' absence, Mentor was responsible for leading the kingdom and for ensuring Telemachus grew to manhood as a competent and successful heir to the throne of Ithaca. Illustrated in the following is this level of responsibility:

> Early in the poem, we are informed that Odysseus had chosen one of his friends to be the overseer of his family and property.... So he spoke and sat down; next Mentor rose to speak, a comrade-in-arms of noble Odysseus. To him the king had committed his entire household, when he sailed off to Troy; he had ordered everyone to obey the old man, trusting that he would keep all things steadfast and undisturbed. (Dova, 2012)

Mentor's role, true to his namesake, elevated him to a higher status and role, and forever positively influenced behavioral science. Mentor's acceptance of this responsibility truly allowed Odysseus to walk, rule, and live in the time of giants.

Mentoring Defined

The mentor's role and actions asked, or coerced, to perform define their necessity. For this reason, mentoring is associated with numerous definitions that attempt to explain generalized categories of the actions. According to the Webster Online Dictionary, a mentor is someone that serves as a teacher or trusted counselor (Webster's, 2013). In Air Force Instruction 36-3401, the USAF defines a mentor as "a trusted counselor or guide. Mentoring, therefore, is a relationship in which a person with greater experience and wisdom guides another person to develop both personally and professionally" (HQ USAF/DP, 2000). From a social science perspective, the definition of mentoring is the dyadic relationship between two individuals whose nature changes over time (Kram, 1983). These dyadic relationships can be decisively defined or loosely organized.

Some definitions of mentoring are not traditional definitions, but are instead an explanation of the role-played. The definition of mentoring has stood the test of time, but the roles and requirements have been less steadfast or resolute. For this reason, Allen et al. (2006) does not define the term, but instead identifies a mentor's common role in the workforce:

> Mentors serve as a vital human resource within organizations. They help ensure the transmission of knowledge to others, assist in the development of a competent workforce, and provide a mechanism for organizational learning. However, effectively mentoring others requires a great deal of time and energy on the part of the mentor. Is this a direct quote? If so, use appropriate APA format. (Allen et al. 2006).

The great amounts of time and energy put forth by a mentor is one aspect that helps define the often-prestigious connotation associated with the role. The more mentoring provided, the more time provided by and drain on the mentor (Lentz & Allen, 2009).

The mentoring relationship, whether associated with the provider or recipient, can take place throughout different lifespan periods. For this reason, defined boundaries are necessary for discussion standardization. Distinct streams of mentoring scholarship attempt to encapsulate the events individuals experience at different stages of life. Each compartment segments linear periods in a given lifespan. From the middle of childhood to that of adolescence, primary developmental issues involve learning the cultivation of healthy peer-to-peer relationships, overcoming academic challenges, and developing personal responsibility (Eby et al., 2008). Early in adulthood, transitions revolve around psychological and physical separation from parents, developing close emotional bonds with non-family members, and development of self-identity (Eby et al., 2008). Upon workforce entry, a general focus on developing stable occupational self-image and discovery of societal roles occurs (Eby et al., 2008). These distinct streams of mentoring attempt to compartmentalize the generalized relationship differences between the individuals involved.

Today, the direct and indirect effects of mentoring embrace almost every facet of an individual's personal and professional life. Common examples of mentoring are seen in the relationship between a parental figure and child, little league baseball player and more experienced coach, older sister teaching a younger brother how to dance before prom, high school student and college advisor discussing future endeavors, and a military training instructor and respective trainees learning Air Force culture. Not to mention, mentoring has debuted as a vital dynamic in movies such as George Lucas' *Star Wars.* The relationship between Jedi Master and Padawan expertly illustrates the prevalence of mentors even in the film industry. If prevalently portrayed in movies and the readily seen in other life-growing experiences, it is easily understood how mentoring as a theme has illustrated its necessity in modern society and for the advancement of professional and personal goals.

Mentoring in the USAF

For individuals associated with the USAF, a common example of the mentor-protégé relationship may be portrayed in the interactions between a Logistics Readiness Squadron (LRS) Commander, typically in the rank of Major (Maj) or Lieutenant Colonel (Lt Col), and Mission Support Group (MSG) Commander, traditionally in the rank of Colonel. In this context, the far more experienced MSG Commander imparts past examples of actions taken, experiences, and mistakes made so the lower grade LRS Commander may learn from these examples. These examples aid the LRS Commander in learning without making the same mistakes.

Seldom one comes across an idea that is enveloping and rational, but feebly comprehended by the intended audience. Arguably, mentoring in the USAF is one such occurrence. On 1 November 1996, the USAF formalized Air Force Policy Directive (AFPD) 36-34. This directive solidified the USAF's dedication and resolve for the mentoring of its Airmen. This solidification did not fully derive from its own status. The governing regulation and implementation authority for AFPD 36-34 resided in Air Force Instruction (AFI) 36-3401. As an introduction to AFPD 36-34, it states:

> This instruction implements Air Force Policy Directive (AFPD) 36-34, *Air Force Mentoring Program.* It provides guidance on how to carry out Air Force Mentoring, which was established to bring about a cultural change in the way we view professional

development. Mentoring is an essential ingredient in developing well-rounded, professional, and competent future leaders. The goal of this instruction is to help each person reach his or her full potential, thereby enhancing the overall professionalism of the Air Force. (HQ USAF/DP, 2000)

In 2000, updates to both AFPD 36-34 and AFI 36-3401 finalized and further explained mentoring expectations in the context of the USAF. Easily understood, the intent of F. Whitten Peters, then Secretary of the Air Force (SECAF), was to " ...infuse all levels of leadership with mentoring to affect a culture change -- one where officers, NCOs, and civilians can pass on the principles, traditions, shared values, and lessons of our profession" (HQ USAF/DPDE, 2000). The SECAF's approach was lofty, but logical approach to strengthening USAF culture and ensuring continued Air and Space dominance.

At times, both mentor and protégé may be unaware of their relationship status and this can cause problems later. Especially in the USAF, the degree to which a mentoring relationship is official versus unofficial is truly indistinguishable at times. In many instances, an Airman may believe they do not have a mentor when in essence their supervisor or higher-ranking officemate, that just so happens to have taken an interest in the advancement of their career, provides guidance at the wrong time or when not convenient. Imparting of guidance based on life or previous work experiences may go unrecognized as mentorship due to the timing or method in which presented.

In time, the official and unofficial protégés of today's USAF become the mentors of tomorrow. As protégés become mentors and find themselves in positions of influence, it follows that they will wield social influence and power (Blass & Ferris, 2007). AFPD 36-34 (2000) designates Air Force supervisors as mentors; no longer is it solely the responsibility of company grade officers. All supervisors in the USAF, military and civilians alike, are responsible for providing career guidance to their Airmen, ensuring professional development, knowledge of air and space power, understanding Air Force history and heritage, the ethos of air warrior profession, and the Air Force's core values of integrity, service, and excellence (HQ USAF/DP, 2000). Mentors should focus on the protégés' technical competence as well as developing their adaptive capacity in order to prepare them for future leadership endeavors (Blass & Ferris, 2007). This passing of the torch ensures a passing of culture between generations of Airmen.

The relationship between mentors and protégés in the USAF may vary greatly depending on their respective personal experiences and backgrounds. Whether or not an initial relationship crystallizes into one of a mentor-protégé depends on a number of elements such as individual's characteristics, career factors, environmental factors, and the type of relationship (Blass & Ferris, 2007). These perspectives can determine the mentoring expectations for both individuals involved in the relationship. Mentors and protégé can have different experiences in and reactions to mentoring because each occupies a unique role in the relationship (Eby, Durley, Evans, & Ragins, 2008). As with any corporation or business, the supervisors within have different styles of leadership. Micromanagers tend to breed other micromanagers, whereas leaders that champion empowerment may take a less intrusive approach and generate empowered leaders. Certain Airmen take offense to being micromanaged, while others may enjoy the closeness of supervision. These differences in the mentor-protégé relationship can be the differentiating factors between positively and negatively perceived mentoring experiences.

Mentors must strike a careful balance between being overly supportive of their protégés and yet willing to provide constructive criticism and feedback (Eby et al., 2008). Charged with mentoring, supervisors in the USAF advance their protégé's knowledge on principles, traditions, shared values, and lessons of the USAF profession of arms (HQ USAF/DPDE, 2000). Overly supportive supervisors may hinder personal growth of the protégé and an unwillingness to provide criticism can distort the chain of command. Supervisors may be reluctant to perform the role of a mentor if recently promoted from the same rank as a subordinate, worry more about friendships, or are unsure of their leadership capability. In the Air Force, leadership capability takes time to develop. The enlisted Noncommissioned Officer Academy and officer Aerospace Basic Course attempt to impart the groundwork, but natural ability and experience often cultivate true ability. Meeting a careful balance fully optimizes the possibilities of the mentoring relationship for both Airmen involved.

Imparting guidance is a key aspect of any mentoring relationship. This is especially true within the strict constructs of the Unites States Armed Forces. The avenue at which this information passes depends on the relationship's circumstances. You could not expect a scuba master and open-water diving protégé to have full-blown verbal counseling session 100 feet below the water's surface could you? In the military, the avenue in question often resembles a formal or informal counseling session, or an order or series of orders. In any mentoring relationship, feedback is a critical element for both the mentor and mentored. The following excerpt paints a vivid image of this expectation:

> Mentoring is a communicative process. It is not a method for shooting information at a person who writes down every word. The ideal mentor is not a guru perched motionless atop a remote Himalayan mountain peak, sitting with legs folded and naval in mind, dispensing wisdom periodically like a fortunetelling vending machine. Mentoring involves genuine two-way communication between mentor and protégé on a protracted, continuing basis. (Kinich, 2001)

Too often, the perception of mentors is that they are perched atop a mountain talking down to their disciples. To desire only one-way feedback is detrimental to the sanctity of the mentorship program. One-way feedback is prevalent in the USAF and often drives Airman to pull away from more experienced, higher-ranking supervisors, leadership, or officemates. To have Airmen pulling away from a vital program such as this is detrimental to the growth of USAF members and the overarching culture.

Established in 1996, nearly twenty years later, the USAF mandated mentorship program remains unknown to many Airmen and not yet fully implemented. Despite not attaining full implementation and unfamiliar, many Airmen still crave mentorship and a better understanding of their profession of arms. This desire for understanding demonstrates itself in the willingness not only to accomplish assigned jobs and the designated mission, but also to do them well. The perceived notions of Airmen, in the overarching areas of stress, retention (turn over intent), job satisfaction, and organizational commitment illustrate this lofty point.

Defining Stress, Retention (Turn-Over Intent), Job Satisfaction, and Organizational Commitment

Keinan (1997) defines stress in three categories: Stress as stimulation -- stress is a powerful stimulation that combines characteristics of loss and threat; Stress as reaction -- stress is a reaction to a particular event; Stress as relation -- stress that pertains to the interaction between the person and environment. Depending on the type of situation, the definition of stress will vary. For instance, waiting on a promotion announcement can be very stressful, but it is an anticipatory good stress. Whereas, bad stress is often associated with awaiting punishment for an offense or infraction, and can have negative effects on the individual's perception. Stress is a personal stimulus that affects each employee differently and therefore influences their perception of the event differently; different people handle stress very differently (Chun, Sosik, & Yun, 2012).

The definition of Retention is the act of retaining something or holding or keeping materials in possession, usually in a desired state or condition, as opposed to disposing of them (Webster's, 2013). Neither of these definitions fully explains retention as relevant to a workforce, but do allow for general understanding of the concept. The perception of retention, or better described as turn over intent, better exhibits the possibly of an Airmen staying in the USAF. Merriam-Webster (2013) defines turnover as "the number of persons hired within a period to replace those leaving or dropped from a workforce; *also*: the ratio of this number to the number in the average force maintained." Turn over intent is defined as the intent to leave one's job, organization, or career (de Tormes Eby, 2012).

One definition of job satisfaction states it is a pleasurable or positive emotional understanding derived from the appraisal of a job (Hsu, 2011). Another definition states, Job satisfaction is "typically a multi-item self-report measure of how happy one is with one's career or how successful an individual believes he or she has been in his or her career to date" (Allen, Eby, Poteet, Lentz, & Lima, 2004). Judge, Hulin, & Dalal (2009) defines job satisfaction as a multidimensional psychological response to one's job in which responses have cognitive or evaluative, and affective or emotional components. Conversely defined, job dissatisfaction is:

> A job is not something we think of only occasionally, as most do about religion, capital punishment, an honor system on campus, people of another race or country, or donating blood. We experience jobs on a nearly constant basis during our working hours; stress caused by job dissatisfaction is our constant companion at work and even on daily commutes. (Judge et al., 2009)

The definition of job dissatisfaction above also incorporates aspects of stress of which was defined in the previous paragraph.

For this research effort, the definition of organizational commitment derived by Bruce Buchanan will serve as a baseline. He defines it as the emotional connection to a particular organization and characterizes employee attitudes towards the organization into three generalized considerations: "Identification, internalization of the organization's goals and values; Involvement, activity that employees perform as part of their roles; Loyalty, a sense of belonging to the employing organization" (Buchanan, 1974). Another definition describes it as emotional attachment to an organization, identification with an organization, and involvement with the organization (Chun et al., 2012). Organizational commitment represents a more encompassing idea than just sheer loyalty because it represents a relationship between employee and organization in which the health of the organization is a priority to the individual or individuals (Mowday, Porter, & Steers, 1982).

Perceived Notions of Mentoring

Traditional predictors, such as job stress (Michael, Court, & Petal, 2009), turnover intention (Holtom, Mitchell, Lee, & Eberly, 2008; Smith, Holtom, & Mitchell, 2011), job satisfaction (Judge & Saari, 2004; Michael et al., 2009), and organizational commitment (Chun, 2012) dominate organizational behavior literature. While some researchers have begun to scrutinize the impact perceived notions of mentoring in comparison to non-mentoring on these variables. These variables, although well used in academia, youth, and commercial work related research efforts (Eby et al., 2008) have rarely, if at all, been used to compare the perceptions of mentored and non-mentored Airmen in the USAF. Positive affluence in these generalized categories can differentiate the perceptions of mentored and non-mentored Airmen. Research has indicated employees who receive mentoring experience added promotions, have higher incomes overall, and are more satisfied with respective pay and benefits (Ensure & Murphy, 1997).These areas can be further broken down into varying categories that concern overall stress, retention (turn over intent), job satisfaction, and organizational commitment of our dedicated Airmen.

Stress has negative and positive effects on employees in both the commercial sector and U.S. Military (Langley, 2012). With obvious differences between the commercial and military sector, most work environments have both good and bad stressors. Mentors are capable of assisting with stress management in these type environments (Military Leadership Diversity Commission, 2010). For instance, in the retail industry perceived coworker involvement and supervisory support serve to reduce work stress and enhance job satisfaction among employees (Hsu, 2011). Without a mentor's mediation, negative stressors can highly influence a protégé's perception of short and long-term self-efficacy (Judge, Hurst, & Simon, 2009).

The presence of psychological strain and stress appear unavoidable to most employees in increasingly demanding, competitive, and diverse work environments. Mentoring may provide a means by which protégés can exercise control over the challenges of the situation (Chun et al., 2012). Hsu (2011) noted previous studies have shown that employees with greater degrees of internal locus of control typically cope better in stressful situations than employees with higher external locus of control. Similarly, a pool of accounting professionals surveyed in Taiwan illustrated that individuals with higher levels of internal locus of control more often have lower levels of job stress (Chen & Silverthorne, 2008). This additional help may encourage protégés to have a positive perception when facing a situation that appears insurmountable or give a stress reduction advantage over those individuals with mentors. In accordance with the research objective and these observations, the first research hypothesis is:

Hypothesis 1: On average, mentored Airmen perceive themselves to have lower levels of overall stress associated with the requirements of a military way of life.

From a managerial and leadership perspective, retention (turn over intent) of high-quality employees is more important today than it has ever been before (Holtom et al., 2008). Additionally, Holtom et al. (2008) proclaim that a number of controversial trends (e.g., globalization, increase in knowledge work, accelerating rate of technological advancement) make it vital for firms to retain human capital. Behavioral outcomes associated with turnover intentions are intimately related to perceptions of mentoring (de Tormes Eby, 2012). In the teaching system, effective mentoring support has shown to help increase retention (Hallam, Chou, Hite, & Hite, 2012). This is largely because academic mentoring tends to target student retention (Eby et al., 2008). This association is likely associated with first-term Airmen as well, although there is no documentation to back this statement. Yet, literature suggests several benefits of good mentoring include retention (Hallam et al., 2012).

The following chart exhibits annual total separation rates for generalized industry sectors; this chart does not account for seasonality of separations. Of note are the high separation rates of federal employees during the years of 2001-2007:

Industry and region	2001	2002	2003	2004	2005	2006	2007	2008
Total...	49 8	46 3	44 5	45 4	46 4	46 0	45 1	43.3
INDUSTRY								
Total private.................................	55 7	51 9	49 8	50 7	52 0	51 2	50 1	48.7
Mining and Logging............................	46 0	44 4	47 2	44 3	40 3	37 4	43 0	43.2
Construction..................................	79 4	77 2	75 8	73 6	74 8	67 9	65 2	72.7
Manufacturing.................................	38 6	35 9	33 7	32 7	32 5	33 6	35 1	33.3
Durable goods	36 0	34 9	33 4	32 0	32 2	30 8	32 7	31.8
Nondurable goods............................	42 9	37 6	34 3	33 8	33 1	38 4	39 2	35.9
Trade, transportation, and utilities..........	53 7	48 9	47 6	50 4	51 2	51 2	48 4	47.3
Wholesale trade	36 6	35 2	34 1	34 3	33 2	32 1	35 3	35.1
Retail trade................................	64 1	58 0	55 8	59 4	60 4	62 0	57 5	54.9
Transportation, warehousing, and utilities ..	41 9	37 0	37 8	41 2	43 7	40 5	36 0	38.9
Information...................................	46 7	40 0	34 2	33 3	35 2	37 5	32 9	29.9
Financial activities..........................	35 6	33 4	31 4	34 1	33 3	35 4	39 3	35.2
Finance and insurance.......................	32 6	28 6	25 8	28 6	28 8	30 3	35 6	30.9
Real estate and rental and leasing...........	44 2	47 0	47 5	49 8	45 7	49 8	49 7	47.6
Professional and business services	73 9	72 4	64 8	64 8	67 6	65 0	62 3	60.9
Education and health services.................	35 5	32 8	32 6	31 9	33 2	33 1	32 3	32.1
Educational services	26 2	23 5	28 7	25 1	26 6	28 7	28 9	28.3
Leisure and hospitality	93 0	81 7	80 0	82 3	83 6	82 8	81 5	75.5
Arts, entertainment, and recreation..........	95 7	85 5	87 0	88 6	83 9	77 3	81 3	76.6
Accommodation and food services	92 5	81 0	78 8	81 2	83 5	83 8	81 5	75.3
Other services	44 1	45 7	48 7	48 8	52 4	45 8	46 0	44.6
Government....................................	18 5	18 2	17 7	18 5	17 7	19 1	19 1	15.7
Federal.......................................	18 6	20 2	20 9	19 9	18 4	26 4	30 2	11.6
State and local...............................	18 5	17 9	17 2	18 3	17 6	18 0	17 6	16.3

Figure 1. Annual Industry Separation Rates (US. Dept of Labor, 2009)

If in full effect, could the mentoring program have made a difference for at least the USAF members encompassed by these 18.4-30.2 percentage rates? Although, separation rates in the federal government are far lower than in many other industries.

Inevitably, high turnover rates lead to a shortage of experienced and skilled personnel (Minor, Wells, Angel, & Matz, 2011) and a degradation of mission. Retention of a technical workforce is critical to both the military and the taxpayer, especially as the Air Force moves to acquire increasingly complex systems (Beck, 2005). When left to their own vices or the advice of a peer/coworker, employees may make decisions counter-intuitive to their desired actions.

Studies show that the effect of a perceived supervisor, compared to coworker support, found that perceived supervisor support strongly related to lesser turnover intention as opposed to perceived coworker support (Hsu, 2011). The success of any unit is dependent on retention and may be highly affected by mentorship of Airmen at all stages of their careers. Based on the possible effects of mentoring on retention (intent to stay), the second hypotheses is:

Hypothesis 2: Mentored Airmen, as opposed to non-mentored, on average have greater perceptions of retention (intent to stay) in the USAF.

Research examining affective outcomes such as job satisfaction dominates mentoring literature (Allen, Shockley, & Poteat, 2010; Judge & Saari, 2004). Much of mentoring literature predominantly focuses on the job satisfaction derived by the protégé when engaged in a formal and informal relationship (Allen et al., 2004; Hsu, 2011). Mentorship enables information exchange, knowledge acquisition, and access into social networks that include repositories of knowledge. Because career-related mentoring functions consist of behaviors that prepare the protégé for career advancement, it makes sense the more career-related mentoring provided, the greater the job satisfaction realized (Allen et al., 2004). Airmen more than likely experience this positive phenomenon as well since the military in general provides such rich base due to size, diversity, and worldly scope (Smith et al., 2011), but no research has been found that supports this claim. On the other hand, in the commercial sector and academia there have been numerous research efforts that can support this statement.

In the commercial industry, factors such as professional learning communities influence professional satisfaction derived in the workplace (Hallam et al., 2012). By studying employees of high-tech companies and government agencies, McCalister, Dolbier, Webster, Mallon, &

Steinhardt (2006) examined the extent to which environmental variables (supervisor support) impact work stress and job satisfaction. Results illustrated supervisor support significantly influenced work stress and job satisfaction (McCalister et al., 2006). In another research effort, the relationship between perceived supervisor support and job satisfaction was tested. Experimental results illustrated perceived supervisor support positive effects job satisfaction, suggesting the higher the perceived supervisor support (mentoring), the higher the job satisfaction (Hsu, 2011). In academia, mentoring literature suggests similar results. Mentored undergraduate students have a higher GPA, more units completed per semester, and a lower dropout rate than their non-mentored counterparts (Paglis, Green, & Bauer, 2006). Job satisfaction similarities transcend professions, and ultimately may serve to influence perceptions amongst mentored and non-mentored Airmen as well. Based on the discussed effects of job satisfaction, the third hypothesis for this research effort is:

Hypothesis 3: Mentored Airmen, as opposed to non-mentored, have greater average perceptions of job satisfaction in the USAF.

Organizational commitment is another prevalent affective outcome that dominates the mentoring literature (Allen et al., 2004; Kraimer, Seibert, Wayne, & Liden, 2010; Michael et al., 2009). The samples (constituting "n") in this study derived from numerous other research efforts; in which none of which pertained to Airmen in the USAF. Results from the meta-analysis indicate mentored individuals are perceived to be committed to their career (weighted mean $r = .15$) versus their non-mentored counterparts (Allen et al., 2004). Other studies have shown significant correlations between mentoring and organizational commitment in the short and long-term (Eby, Durley, Evans, & Ragins, 2006). In a regression analysis conducted by

Ensher and Murphy (1997), results indicated that protégés in the beginning stages of their relationships with their mentors reported experiencing significantly fewer challenges with organizational Commitment.

Organizational commitment generally varies depending on the specific employees within the company or industry. Although, what generally drives organizational commitment in employees is often the incentives associated with career satisfaction (Judge & Saari, 2004). Lodged in the back of the mind of many Airmen, is the notion of a 20-plus year retirement pay that increases with realized promotions. For this reason, Holtom et al. (2008) believe enlisted members in the USAF with greater organizational commitment are less likely to leave until meeting their 20-year eligibility requirement. Therefore, viewing organizational commitment through a specific lens to understand how its associated incentives can affect the mentor-protégé relationship is a necessity. Based on the reported correlations between mentoring and organizational commitment, the final hypothesis for this research effort is:

Hypothesis 4: Mentored Airmen, as opposed to non-mentored, on average have a greater perception of organizational commitment than non-mentored in the USAF.

Summary

In sum, the similarities between mentoring in industry (commercial sector), academia, make it reasonable to associate the literature derived from these sources to help shape and inform thinking pertaining to the mentor-protégé relationship in the USAF. Each source illustrates varying similarities that compares commercial industry with the USAF, and how application of mentoring can serve to advance the mentor-protégé relationships. As in the commercial industry, mentoring in the U.S. Air Force can be very beneficial. Mentoring propels the shaping of principles, traditions, shared values, and lessons associated with military profession of arms. These factors are not very different from the literature associated with most private, commercial, and academic environments and settings.

III.   Methodology

Introduction

The focus of this research effort is to determine whether mentoring significantly influences perceived notions of stress, retention, job satisfaction, and organizational commitment amongst active duty Airmen. The quantitative research involved ascertaining whether the perceived benefits of mentoring, in direct opposition to not mentoring, for four USAF career-influencing measures is statistically significant. The following figure depicts the stages utilized to comprise this research effort:

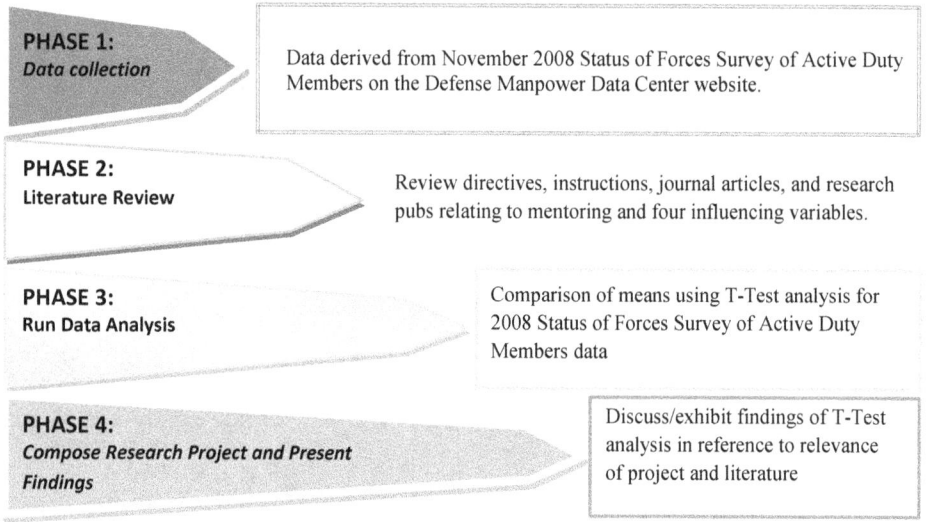

Figure 2: Phases of Research Project

Methodology is included in Phase 3 as part of "running data analysis" due to the fact this chapter describes how the T-Test analysis was run.

Procedure and Participants

The Defense Manpower Data Center collected data for this survey using a 104-item questionnaire administered to U.S. Armed Forces respondents. For this research effort, utilization consisted of specific responses to questions from the November 2008 Status of Forces Survey of Active Duty Members located on the Defense Manpower Data Center (DMDC) website. The entire survey consists of 104 questions and 34,614 random Department of Defense (DoD) participants asked to participate and answer question (87), "In your opinion, have you ever had a mentor?" Of the 34,615 DoD military asked to participate, 26,027 did not return the survey and 1,347 did not answer the question, resulting in a 21% participation rate. Total Airmen surveyed equaled 2,547, in which there was a 98% ± 1% response rate to Question 87 (DMDC, 2009).

Of the total 2,547 eligible Airmen that participated in the November 2008 Status of Forces Survey of Active Duty Members questionnaire, this research effort utilized n = 2,487. Sixty Airmen participants had no numerical values entered in the following individual demographic groups (MENTR, XSEXR, XRETH4R, XMARSTR, YOSCR2, and XPAYGRP2R). The typical respondent was male (n=1937), white (n=1765), married (n=1650), some college or more (n=2259), 10 or more years of active duty service (n=1251), and in the grades of E5-E9 (n=1118). All conditions for Valid Large-Sample Inferences about $(\mu_1 - \mu_2)$ were met: "(1) The two samples are randomly selected in an independent manner from the two target populations. (2) The sample sizes, n_1 and n_2, are both large (i.e., $n_1 \geq 30$ and $n_2 \geq 30$)" (McClave, Benson, & Sincich, 2011). As the samples were both larger than $n = 30$, hypothesis three states

The questionnaire measured 18 overarching dimensions. The 18 overarching dimensions include Eligibility, Satisfaction, Retention, Tempo, Readiness, Stress, Deployments since 11 September 2001, Military OneSource, Impact of Deployments, Organizational

Commitment, Tobacco, Leadership, Organizational Effectiveness, Mentoring, Organizational Culture, Career Opportunities, Permanent Change of Station (PCS) Moves, Taking the Survey and Background Information. Within the Background Information heading, the applicable individual demographic characteristics include Respondent's: Gender, Marital Status, Pay-grade group, Race/Ethnicity, and Years of Active Duty Service. Appendix A includes the questionnaire utilized in this research effort. Appendix B includes the means, standard deviations, reliabilities, and population sizes for all individualized utilized measures.

Measures

Stress. Three items measured stress in this research effort. The first item, number 41, asked participants to indicate, "Overall, how would you rate the current level of stress in your work life?" The second item, number 42, asked respondents to indicate, "Overall, how would you rate the current level of stress in your personal life?" Indications for both responses were on a 5-point likert scale, pooled and recoded ranging from "Much More than Usual" (1) to "Much Less than Usual" (5). The third item, number 43, is comprised of sub-questions A-F. It asked, "In the past month, how often have you: a. Felt nervous and stressed? b. Felt that you were unable to control the important things in your life? c. Been upset because of something that happened unexpectedly? d. Been angered because of things that were outside of your control? e. Felt difficulties were piling up so high that you could not overcome them? f. Found that you could not cope with all of the things you had to do?" Indications for all Question 42 responses were on a 5-point likert scale, pooled and recoded ranging from "Very Often" (1) to "Never" (5). Average responses from all three questions generated a total stress score. The Cronbach's Alpha for the stress measure is .89 (n = 2,411, M = 3.45, SD = .76).

Retention. Three items measured retention in this research effort. The first item, Question 23, asked participants, "Suppose that you have to decide whether to stay on active duty. Assuming you could stay, how likely is it that you would choose to do so?" Indications for responses to Question 23 were on a 5-point likert scale ranging from "Very Unlikely" (1) to "Very Likely" (5). The second item, question 24, asked respondents to indicate, "Does your spouse or significant other think you should stay on or leave active duty?" The third item, question 25, asked respondents to indicate, "Does your family think you should stay on or leave active duty?" Indications for both of the last two questions were on a 5-point likert scale, ranging from "Strongly Favors Leaving" (1) to "Strongly Favors Staying" (5). Average responses from all three questions generated a total retention score. The Cronbach's Alpha for the retention measure is .83 (n = 2,017, M = 3.62, SD = 1.10).

Job Satisfaction. Two items measured job satisfaction in this research effort. The first item, question 20, is comprised of sub-questions A-E. It asked, "Taking all things into consideration, how satisfied are you, in general, with each of the following aspects of being in the military?: a. Your total compensation (i.e., base pay, allowances, and bonuses). b. The type of work you do in your military job. c. Your opportunities for promotion. d. The quality of your coworkers. e. The quality of your supervisor." The second item, number 21, asked participants to indicate, "Overall, how satisfied are you with the military way of life?" Indications for all Question 20 subparts and Question 21 responses were on a 5-point likert scale ranging from "Very Dissatisfied" (1) to "Very Satisfied" (5). Average responses from both questions generated a total job satisfaction score. The Cronbach's Alpha for the job satisfaction measure is .75 (n = 2,408, M = 3.75, SD = .66).

Organizational Commitment. One item measured organizational commitment in this research effort. Question 26, is comprised of sub-questions A-O. It asked, "To what extent do you agree or disagree with the following statements?: a. I enjoy serving in the military. b. Serving in the military is consistent with my personal goals. c. If I left the military, I would feel like I am starting all over again. d. I would feel guilty if I left the military. e. Generally, on a day-to-day basis, I am happy with my life in the military. F. It would be difficult for me to leave the military and give up the benefits that are available in the Service. g. I would not leave the military right now because I have a sense of obligation to the people in it. h. I really feel as if the military's values are my own. i. I would have difficulty finding a job if I left the military. j. Generally, on a day-to-day basis, I am proud to be in the military. k. If I left the military, I would feel like I had let my country down. l. I continue to serve in the military because leaving would require considerable sacrifice. m. I feel like being a member of the military can help me achieve what I want in life. n. One of the problems with leaving the military would be the lack of available alternatives. o. I am committed to making the military my career." Indications for all Question 26 subparts were on a 5-point likert scale ranging from "Strongly disagree" (1) to "Strongly agree" (5). Average responses generated a total organizational commitment score. The Cronbach's Alpha for the organizational commitment measure is .88 (n = 2,369, M = 3.32, SD = .64).

Individual Demographic Characteristics. Survey items 2, 3, 4, 17, and 22 respectively collected data regarding Airmen respondents' Gender, Pay-grade Group, Marital Status, Race/Ethnicity, and Years of Active Duty Service.

Gender. Between the choice of male and female, respondents selected their gender. Responses were coded either 1. (Male) or 2. (Female). (n = 2,487, M = 1.22, SD = .42).

Pay-grade Group. Regarding pay-grade, Question 3 asked participants, "What is your current pay-grade? Mark one." Responses were coded: 1. E1, 2. E2, 3. E3, 4. E5, 5. E5, 6. E6, 7. E7, 8. E8, 9. E9, 21. O1/O1E, 22. O2/O2E, 23. O3/O3E, 24. O4, 25. 05, 26. O6 or above. The Defense Manpower Data Center then recoded variable into five groups. The groups are: 1 = E1-E4, 2 = E5-E9, 3 = W1-W5, 4 = O1-O3, and 5 = O4-O6. (n = 2,487, M = 2.61, SD = 1.42).

Marital Status. With respect to marital status, participants selected their current marital status from the following choices: 1. Married, 2. Separated, 3. divorced, 4. Widowed, 5. never married. (n = 2,487, M = 1.66, SD = .47).

Race/Ethnicity. Regarding Race/Ethnicity, Question 17 asked participants, "What is your race? Mark one or more races to indicate what race you consider yourself to be." Possible boxes to check are: White, Black or African-American, American Indian or Alaska Native, Asian (e.g., Asian Indian, Chinese, Filipino, Japanese, Korean, Vietnamese), and Native Hawaiian or other Pacific Islander (e.g., Samoan, Guamanian or Chamorro). The Defense Manpower Data Center then recoded variable into two collapsed categories/groups. The groups are: 1 = White or 2 = Total Minority. (n = 2,487, M = 1.29, SD = .45).

Years of Active Duty Service. Regarding years of active duty service, Question 22 asked participants, "How many years of active duty service have you completed (including enlisted, warrant officer, and commissioned officer time)? To indicate less than 1 year, enter "0". To indicate 35 years or more, enter "35"." The Defense Manpower Data Center then recoded variable into four groups. The groups are: 1 = Less than 3 years, 2 = 3 to less than 6 years, 3 = 6 years to less than 10 years, 4 = 10 or more years. (n = 2,487, M = 3.03, SD = 1.14).

Validity & Reliability

When discussing the criteria for judging the quality of research designs, there are four commonly utilized tests. These common tests entail assurance of construct validity, internal validity, external validity, and reliability (Yin, 2009). Construct validity attempts to identify the correct operational measures for the concepts studied. Distinguished from spurious relationships, internal validity seeks to establish a causal relationship, where certain conditions can lead to other conditions. External validity attempts to establish a study's findings in a generalized domain. Whereas reliability demonstrates, such as the data collection procedures, that the operations of a study are repeatable with the same or similar results (Yin, 2009). These are the four commonly utilized criteria for judging the quality of research designs.

In order to protect against the threat of internal validly, a few steps were necessary to minimize likelihood. For construct validity, the number of survey takers, "N," for both mentored and non-mentored survey recipients, equaled greater than thirty. In order to control for the internal validity of the study, issued surveys only went to DoD personnel. These controlling measures included Airmen asked to login using a military identification card and through a specific DoD sanctioned survey website. November 2008 surveys solely represented the data utilized in this research effort. As a means to control for internal validity, of the 2,547 USAF members that completed the mentoring questions on the survey, no participant definitively knew their responses might become part of a research effort. In order to protect against the threat of external validly, survey designers replicate the survey every four years with minimal or no change to the content of the questions. Countering threats to reliability included ensuring the location of unmolested survey data is fully protected for all DoD members to access with a common access card. All case study data and survey questions utilized in this research effort are contained within the appendices.

Summary

In summary, the researcher received November 2008 Status of Forces Survey of Active Duty Members data from the Defense Manpower Data Center. With a .95 level of confidence/significance, independent sample t-tests (unpaired t-test) encompassing 2,487 Air Force members were performed comparing population means between sampled data pools. Ratio data, encompassing 1745 mentored and 742 non-mentored Airmen, examined if perceptions differed significantly on concerns of overall stress, retention, job satisfaction, and organizational commitment. The results from the independent sample t-tests analysis follow in Chapter 4.

IV.   Results and Analysis

Preface

In order to compare ratio data from the two independent mentored and non-mentored populations, t-test can distinguish the level of statistical significance difference between responses on the survey. T-tests compare the means of two populations. The following figure illustrates general large-sample procedures for testing hypotheses about the mean:

$$\text{var}(x_o) = \frac{s_e^2}{slope^2} \left(\frac{1}{n} + \frac{n(y_o - \bar{y})^2}{slope^2 S_{xx}} \right),$$

where

$$s_e^2 = \frac{S_{xx}S_{yy} - (S_{xy})^2}{n(n-2)S_{xx}}$$

$$S_{xx} = n\sum_{i=1}^{n}(x_i - \bar{x})^2 \quad \text{and} \quad S_{yy} = n\sum_{i=1}^{n}(y_i - \bar{y})^2 \quad \text{and} \quad S_{xy} = n\sum_{i=1}^{n}(x_i - \bar{x})(y_i - \bar{y})$$

n is the number of points in the regression line, and
x, y points are unacidified values and acidified values, respectively.

Figure 3: Large Sample T-Test (McClave et al., 2011).

Careful considerations should be adhered to for factors associated with the Levene's Test for Equality of Variances (F and significance value), and the T-Test for Equality of Means (t-statistic, degrees of freedom, mean, and standard deviation).

Hypotheses Tests

For each hypothesis test conducted in the study, all conditions for Valid Large-Sample Inferences about (μ_1 - μ_2) were met: "(1) The two samples are randomly selected in an independent manner from the two target populations. (2) The sample sizes, n_1 and n_2, are both large (i.e., $n_1 \geq 30$ and $n_2 \geq 30$)" (McClave et al., 2011). As the samples were both larger than n = 30, hypothesis three states:

Hypothesis 1: On average, mentored Airmen perceive themselves to have lower levels of overall stress associated with the requirements of a military way of life.

For perceived levels of overall stress, appendix 3 illustrates the Levene's Test for Equality of Variances indicated, at α = .05 (F = .02 and p = .88), equal variances are not assumed. For the test statistic, z, the rejection region is $z > z_\alpha$, with z_α = 1.65 (for α = .05) (McClave et al., 2011). Additionally, the p-value (.10) associated with the Test of Equality of Means is greater than α = .05, concluding the average .06 differences between mentored and non-mentored Airmen on perceptions of stress is due to chance. (t = 1.64, df = 1370.30, mean: mentored = 3.47 and non-mentored = 3.41, and SD: mentored = .76 and non-mentored = .75). Thus, the results of this research study do not support hypothesis 1.

Hypothesis 2: Mentored Airmen, as opposed to non-mentored, on average have greater perceptions of retention (intent to stay) in the USAF.

For perceptions of retention, appendix 3 illustrates the Levene's Test for Equality of Variances indicated, at α = .05 (F = .01 and p = .94), equal variances are not assumed. Yet, when utilizing the p-value in the t-test for Equality of Means, it illustrates a different scenario. For the test statistic, z, the rejection region is $z > z_\alpha$, with z_α = 1.65 (for α = .05) (McClave et al., 2011). The p-value (.00) of the test is less than α = .05, concluding the average .26 differences between mentored and non-mentored Airmen on perceptions of retention is not due to chance. (t = 4.78, df = 1034.33, mean: mentored = 3.69 and non-mentored = 3.43, and SD: mentored = 1.09

and non-mentored = 1.09). Thus, the results of this research study support the hypothesis that mentored Airmen on average have greater perceptions of retention in the USAF.

Hypothesis 3: Mentored Airmen, as opposed to non-mentored, have greater average perceptions of job satisfaction in the USAF.

For perceptions of job satisfaction, appendix 3 illustrates the Levene's Test for Equality of Variances indicated, at α = .05 (F = 2.84 and p = .09), equal variances are not assumed. On the other hand, when utilizing the p-value in the t-test for Equality of Means, the results illustrate a very different situation. For the test statistic, z, the rejection region is $z > z_\alpha$, with z_α = 1.65 (for α = .05) (McClave et al., 2011). The p-value (.00) for the test of Equality of Means is less than α = .05, concluding the average .20 differences between mentored and non-mentored Airmen on perceptions of job satisfaction is not due to chance. (t = 6.79, df = 1299.29, mean: mentored = 3.81 and non-mentored = 3.60, and SD: mentored = .65 and non-mentored = .67). Ergo, the results of this study support the hypothesis that mentored Airmen on average have greater perceptions of job satisfaction in the USAF.

Hypothesis 4: Mentored Airmen, as opposed to non-mentored, on average have a greater perception of organizational commitment than non-mentored in the USAF.

For the average Airmen's perceptions of organizational commitment, appendix 3 illustrates the Levene's Test for Equality of Variances indicated, at α = .05 (F = .08 and p = .79), equal variances are not assumed. Yet, when utilizing the p-value in the t-test for Equality of Means, it illustrates there is a recognizable level of significance. The p-value (.00) for the test of Equality of Means illustrated a less than α = .05 level of significance, concluding the average

.128 differences between mentored and non-mentored Airmen on perceptions of organizational commitment is not due to chance. (t = 4.48, df = 1325.13, mean: mentored = 3.36 and non-mentored = 3.23, and SD: mentored = .63 and non-mentored = .63). Thus, the results of this research support hypothesis 4 showing that mentored Airmen in the USAF on average have greater perceptions of organizational commitment than those that are non-mentored.

Summary

This chapter summarizes the findings of analyses conducted on the November 2008 Status of Forces Survey of Active Duty Members data collected from the Defense Manpower Data Center. The hypotheses were evaluated using t-test analysis testing for average differences in the means. With a .95 level of confidence, independent sample t-tests (unpaired t-test) encompassing 2,487 USAF Airmen were performed to compare population means between the sampled data pools. Ratio data, 1,745 mentored and 742 non-mentored Airmen, examined whether perceptions differed significantly on concerns of overall stress, retention (turn over intent), job satisfaction, and organizational commitment. The results demonstrated a significant difference between the average perceptions of mentored in comparison to non-mentored Airmen in the areas of retention (turn over intent), job satisfaction, and organizational commitment. Yet, the results indicate there was not a significant difference between the average perceptions of mentored in comparison to non-mentored Airmen when dealing with stress.

V.   Discussion

The purpose of this study was to analyze mentoring and the perceived benefits it has on stress levels, job satisfaction, organizational commitment, and retention in a USAF environment. The derived data came from the November 2008 Status of Forces Survey of Active Duty Members located on the Defense Manpower Data Center website. This study utilized an independent sample t-test to analyze perceived influences on mentored and non-mentored Airmen. This research effort is unique in that no previous published USAF research has focused solely on the impacts of mentoring in association with these variables. Considering the numerous research efforts accomplished in other non-military work environments, this analysis is long overdue.

Results suggest that on average, mentored Airmen have perceived higher levels of retention (H2), job satisfaction (H3), and organizational commitment (H4), whilst perceptions of stress (H1) is minimally, if at all, influenced by mentoring relationships. In reference to the stress variable, similar non-USAF studies have found it to be significant. For instance, Michael et al. (2009) considers stress as a traditional predictor that dominates organizational behavior literature, and Eby et al. (2008) acknowledged the increased frequency in which academia, youth, and commercial work related research efforts utilize stress as a variable. Despite the fact that stress is non-significant in this study, the other three variables (retention, job satisfaction, and organizational commitment) are significant and this aligns with results found in non-USAF studies.

In this study, mentoring may not have had a profound influence on perceptions of stress due to social desirability bias. As Airmen, the respondents of the November 2008 Status of

Forces Survey of Active Duty Members questionnaire possibly answered in a manner that would keep them from notice or identified in a negative manner. The negative connotation or even direct consequences associated with the inability to handle the stress associated with a job (over-stressed) could be the difference between staying "blue" and medical separation. It is impractical to know for sure if social desirability bias had an effect on the respondents in this questionnaire, but it is feasible and therefore worth mentioning as a possibility.

Implications

 Practical Implications. The practical implications include exploiting the results of this study to enhance the knowledge and execution of the current mentoring program. On average, Airmen with higher perceptions of retention, job satisfaction, and organizational commitment are by definition going to stay in the Air Force longer, be more satisfied with their jobs, and be committed to their present organizations. This research effort's results can be included or referenced in AFI 36-3401 and AFD 36-34 as justification for support of the USAF Mentoring Program. Additionally, the results of this study further edify the need for the Defense Manpower Data Center's Status of Forces Survey of Active Duty Members questionnaires. These questionnaires serve to further our knowledge of those we work for, with, and ultimately serve.

 Theoretical Implications. This research effort enables Air Force senior leaders, social behavioral scientist, and DoD critics/enthusiast to better understand the significance of mentoring of active duty USAF members. Additionally, it illustrates the perceived influence mentoring has on career-success variables such as overall retention (turn over intent), job satisfaction, and organizational commitment. With analyzed data to support a better understanding the perceived benefits of mentoring have, USAF senior leaders may better understand the positive influence of mentoring. In turn, senior leaders can ensure that Airmen have the opportunity to request mentors as desired. This simple feat allows for the formal framework for the passing of experience based on professional knowledge in a more standardized manner. Ultimately, this research effort will illustrate how mentoring on a truly required basis may propel the expectation and capability of accomplishing more with less in a fiscally constrained work environment.

Limitations

The Status of Forces Survey of Active Duty Members requests participation of Department of Defense (DoD) service members on a revolving annual basis in which only certain areas of study or matrices are considered. For example, the research variable questions associated with this project (stress, retention, job satisfaction, and organizational commitment) are included in the survey only every four years (2000, 2004, 2008, etc.). Additionally, through the given 4-year cycle, the matrix questions were divided over the three quarters. For this reason, the researcher included only the most recent data available (November 2008) for the scope of this analysis.

Future Research

Since mentoring has proven to be a viable predictor of perceived organizational commitment, job satisfaction, and retention, future research efforts should attempt to sample from a larger population of military personnel; possibly the entire DoD population involving Air Force, Army, Navy and Marines. A larger DoD population could improve generalizability of results across the entire United States military spectrum and not solely the Air Force. With a larger more diverse population, the results may be more encompassing and the stress variable significance may reflect results more aptly associated with numerous commercial research efforts.

Another future research effort could involve a longitudinal study encompassing mentoring and the same variables (stress, retention, job satisfaction, and organizational commitment) comparing 2004 data with 2008 data; or any other years available through the Defense Manpower Data Center website. This could include only USAF members or the entire DoD military population. A longitudinal study may provide results useful in potentially demonstrating a causal relationship between these variables. This proposed study would provide an assessment of the perceptions of Air Force members or DoD personnel at two different points in time; as groups or certain individuals can be tracked by pins. In order to examine the impact of mentoring in comparison to this research, future studies conducted should utilize similar resources and analysis.

Conclusions

The purpose of this study was to analyze mentoring and it perceived benefits on stress levels, job satisfaction, organizational commitment, and retention in a USAF environment. On 1 November 1996, when the USAF formalized Air Force Policy Directive 36-34, it illustrated senior leadership's dedication and resolve for Airmen mentoring. The Secretary of the Air Force intended for all supervisors to take on the role of mentor to pass on USAF principles, traditions, shared values, and lessons. The results of this study do not specifically talk to the role of the mentor, but they do illustrate that for three of the four variables Airmen realize the perceived benefits. Our Airmen realize the benefits, and maybe it is time for a greater level of support of the mentorship program.

Based on this research effort's findings, many opportunities exist in which the USAF can utilize these results to ascertain the worth of mentoring and encourage full usage of the technique. Active support, in addition to the 1996 mandate, could positively influence USAF culture and enable the passing principles, traditions, shared values, and lessons. The results of this effort will assist in proving the worth of mentoring to unbelieving senior, mid-level, and junior supervisors. Understandably, during a time when both budgets and time are constrained, a heightened level of support is costly, but the perceived benefits of mentoring on job satisfaction, organizational commitment, and retention in a U.S. Air Force could be exponential. In combination with future research efforts, this research effort will hopefully encourage the USAF to enact cultural change for the betterment of all members.

Bibliography

Allen, T. D. (2006). Career Success Outcomes Associated With Mentoring Others. *Journal of Career Development, 32(3)*, 272-285.

Allen, T. D., Eby, L. T., & Lentz, E. (2006). Mentorship Behaviors and Mentorship Quality Associated with Formal Mentoring Programs: Closing the Gap Between Research and Practice. *Journal of Applied Psychology, 91*(3), 567-578.

Allen, T. D., Eby, L. T., O'Brien, K. E., & Lentz, E. (2008). The State of Mentoring Research: A Qualitative Review of Current Research Methods and future Research Implications. *Journal of Vocational Behavior, 73*, 343-357.

Allen, T. D., Eby, L. T., Poteet, M. L., Lentz, E., & Lima, L. (2004). Career Benefits Associated With Mentoring for Proteges: A Meta-Analysis. *Journal of Applied Psychology, 89*(1), 127-136.

Allen, T. D., Shockley, K. M., & Poteat, L. (2010). Protege Anxiety Attachment and Feedback in Mentoring Relationships. *Journal of Vocational Behavior, 77*, 73-80.

Beck, D. W. (2005). *An Analysis of Retention Issues of Scientists, Engineers, and Program Managers in the US Air Force.* Cambridge, MA: Retrieved from Massachusetts Institute of Technology.

Blass, F. R., & Ferris, G. R. (2007). Leader Reputation, The Role of Mentoring, Political Skill, Contextual Learning, and Adaptation. *Human Resource Management, Spring*, 5-19.

Buchanan, B. I. (1974). Building Organizational Commitment: The Socialization of Managers in Work Organizations. *Administrative Science Quarterly, 19*, 533-546.

Carruthers, J. (1992). Viewpoint: Who benefits? *Mentoring International, 6*, Pg 48.

Chen, J., & Silverthorne, C. (2008). The impact of locus of control on job stress, job performance and job satisfaction in Taiwan. *Leadership & Organization Development Journal, 29*(7), 572-582.

Chun, J. U., Sosik, J. J., & Yun, N. Y. (2012). A longitudinal Study of Mentor and Protege Outcomes in Formal Mentoring Relationships. *Journal of Organizational Behavior, 33*, 1071-1094.

de Tormes Eby, L. T. (2012). An Interdisciplinary Meta-Analysis of the Potential Antecedents, Correlates, and Consequences of Prote´ge´ Perceptions of Mentoring. *Psychological Bulletin*, 1-36.

DMDC. (2009). *November 2008 Status of Forces Survey of Active Duty Members: Tabulations of Responses.* Department of Defense. Arlington: Defense Manpower Data Center.

Dova, S. (2012). *"Kind Like a Father": On Mentors and Kings in the Odyssey.* The Center for Hellenic Studies. http://chs.harvard.edu/wa/pageR?tn=ArticleWrapper&bdc=12&mn=4351.

Eby, L. T., Allen, T. D., Evans, S. C., Thomas, N., & Du Bois, D. L. (2008). Does mentoring matter? A mutidisciplinary meta-analysis comparing mentored and non-mentored individuals. *Journal of Vocational Behavior, 72,* 254-267.

Eby, L. T., Durley, J. R., Evans, S. C., & Ragins, B. R. (2006). The relationship between short-term mentoring benefits and long-term mentor outcomes. *Journal of Vocational Behavior, 69,* 424-444.

Eby, L. T., Durley, J. R., Evans, S. C., & Ragins, B. R. (2008). Mentors' Perceptions of Negative Mentoring Experiences: Scale Development and Nomological Validation. *Journal of Applied Psychology, 93*(92), 358-373.

Ensure, E. A., & Murphy, S. E. (1997). Effects of Race, Gender, Perceived Similarity, and Contact on Mentor Relationships. *Journal of Vocational Behavior, 50,* 460-481.

Hallam, P. R., Chou, P. N., Hite, J. M., & Hite, S. J. (2012). Two Contrasting Models for Mentoring as They Affect Retention of Beggining Teachers. *NASSP Bulletin, 96*(3), 243-278.

Holtom, B. C., Mitchell, T. R., Lee, T. W., & Eberly, M. (2008). Turnover and Retention Research: A Glance at the Past, a Closer Review of the Present, and a Venture into the Future. *The Academy of Management Annals, 2*(1), 231-273.

HQ USAF/DPDE. (2000). *AIR FORCE INSTRUCTION 36-3401.* Retrieved April 20, 2013, from Air Force E-Publishing: http://static.e-publishing.af.mil/production/1/af_a1/publication/afi36-3401/afi36-3401.pdf.

HQ USAF/DPDE. (2000). *Air Force Policy Directive 36-34, Air Force Mentoring Program.* (U. S. Force, Producer) Retrieved April 21, 2013, from http://webapp1.dlib.indiana.edu/cgi-bin/virtcdlib/index.cgi/821003/FID3/pubs/af/36/afpd36-34/afpd36-34.pdf.

Hsu, Y. R. (2011). Work-family conflict and job satisfaction in stressful working environments. *International Journal of Manpower, 32*(2), 233-248.

Judge, T. A., & Saari, L. M. (2004). Employee Attitudes and Job Satisfaction. *Human Resource Management, Winter,* 395-407.

Judge, T. A., Hulin, C. L., & Dalal, R. S. (2009). Job Satisfaction and Job Effect. *The Oxford Handbook of Industrial and Organizational Psychology*, 2-89.

Judge, T. A., Hurst, C., & Simon, L. S. (2009). Does It Pay to Be Smart, Attractive, or Confident (or All Three)? Relationships Among General Mental Ability, Physical Attractiveness, Core Self-Evaluations, and Income. *Journal of Applied Psychology, 94*(3), 742-755.

Keinan, G. (1997). *Stress Situations: Ways of Coping and Therapy.* Rosh Ha'ain: Prolog Press.

Kinich, J. C. (2001). Leadership and the Art of Mentoring: Tool Kit for the Time Machine. *Journal of Leadership, (Reprint in AU-24, Concepts for Air Force), 1*(2), 123.

Kraimer, M. L., Seibert, S. E., Wayne, S. J., & Liden, R. C. (2010). Antecedents and Outcomes of Organizational Support for Development: The Critical Role of Career Opportunities. *Journal of Applied Psychology, 96*(3), 485-500.

Kram, K. E. (1983). Phases of the Mentor Relationship. *Academy of Management Journal, 26*(4), 608-625.

Langley, J. K. (2012). Occupational Burnout and Retention of Air Force Distributed Common Ground System (DCGS) Intelligence Personnel . Pardee RAND Graduate School. RAND.

Lentz, E., & Allen, T. D. (2009). The Role of Mentoring Others in the Career Plateauing Phenomenon. *Group & Organization Management, 34*(3), 358-384.

McCalister, K. T., Dolbier, C. L., Webster, J. A., Mallon, M. W., & Steinhardt, M. A. (2006). Hardiness and Support at Work as Predictors of Work Stress and Job Satisfaction. *American Journal of Health Promotion, 20*(3), 183-191.

McClave, J. T., Benson, P. G., & Sincich, T. (2011). *Statistics for Business and Economics* (11 ed.). Boston, MA: Prentice Hall Press.

Mentoring. (2013). In *Merriam-Webster Online*. Retrieved from http://www.merriam-webster.com/dictionary/turnover.

Michael, O., Court, D., & Petal, P. (2009). Job Stress and Organizational Commitment Among Mentoring Coordinators. *International Journal of Educational Management, 23*(3), 266-287.

Military Leadership Diversity Commission. (2010). Mentoring Programs Across the Services. 1-6. Arlington, VA. Retrieved from HTTP://mldc.whs.mil/.

Minor, K. I., Wells, J. B., Angel, E., & Matz, A. K. (2011). Predictors of Early Job Turnover Among Juvenile Correctional Facility Staff. *Criminal Justice Review, 36*(1), 58-75.

Mowday, R. T., Porter, L. W., & Steers, R. M. (1982). *Employee-organization linkages: The psychology of commitment, absenteeism, and turnover.* New York: Academic Press.

Paglis, L. L., Green, S. G., & Bauer, T. N. (2006). Does Advisor Mentoring Add Value? A longitudinal Study of Mentoring and Doctoral Student Outcomes. *Research in Higher Education, 47*(4), 451-476.

Smith, D. R., Holtom, B. C., & Mitchell, T. R. (2011). Enhancing Precision in the Prediction of Voluntary Turn-over and retirement. *Journal of Vocational Behavior, 79*, 290-302.

US. Dept of Labor. (2009). *U.S. Bureau of Labor Statistics: Economic News Release.* Retrieved April 5, 2013, from Job Openings and Labor Turnover Survey News Release: http://www.bls.gov/news.release/archives/jolts_03102009.htm

Retention. (2013). In *Merriam-Webster Online.* Retrieved from http://www.merriam-webster.com/dictionary/retention.

Mentoring. (2013). In *Merriam-Webster Online.* Retrieved from http://www.merriam-webster.com/dictionary/mentoring.

Yin, R. K. (2009). *Case Study Research: Design and Methods* (4th ed., Vol. 5). Thousand Oaks, CA, USA: Sage Publications.

Appendix A: November 2008 Status of Forces Survey
of Active Duty Members Questionnaire

ELIGIBILITY

1. In what Service were you on active duty on November 4, 2008?

- Army
- Navy
- Marine Corps
- Air Force
- None, I have separated or retired

BACKGROUND INFORMATION

2. Are you . . . ?

- Male
- Female

3. What is your current paygrade? *Mark one.*

E-1	E-6	W-1	O-1/O-1E
E-2	E-7	W-2	O-2/O-2E
E-3	E-8	W-3	O-3/O-3E
E-4	E-9	W-4	O-4
E-5		W-5	O-5
			O-6 or above

4. What is your marital status?

- Married
- Separated
- Divorced
- Widowed
- Never married

5. **How many years have you been in a relationship with your current significant other (that is, your girlfriend or boyfriend)?**

- ☐ Does not apply; I do not have a girlfriend/boyfriend
- ☐ Less than 1 year
- ☐ 1 year to less than 6 years
- ☐ 6 years to less than 10 years
- ☐ 10 years or more

In the following section, you will be asked questions about your spouse's employment status in enough detail to ensure comparability with national employment surveys.

---

6. **Is your spouse currently serving on active duty (not a member of the National Guard or Reserve)?**
- ☐ Yes
- ☐ No

7. **Is your spouse currently serving as a member of the National Guard or Reserve in a full-time, active duty program (AGR/FTS/AR)?**
- ☐ Yes
- ☐ No

8. **Is your spouse currently serving as a member of another type of National Guard or Reserve unit (e.g., drilling unit, Individual Mobilization Augmentee (IMA), Individual Ready Reserve (IRR))?**
- ☐ Yes
- ☐ No

9. <u>Last week</u>, did your spouse do <u>any</u> work for pay or profit? *Mark "Yes" even if your spouse worked only one hour, or helped without pay in a family business or farm for 15 hours or more.*

☐ Yes

☐ No

10. <u>Last week</u>, was your spouse <u>temporarily</u> absent from a job or business?

☐ Yes, on vacation, temporary illness, labor dispute, etc.

☐ No

11. **Has your spouse been looking for work during the last 4 weeks?**
    - ☐ Yes
    - ☐ No

12. **Last week, could your spouse have started a job if offered one, or returned to work if recalled?**
    - ☐ Yes, could have gone to work
    - ☐ No, because of his/her temporary illness
    - ☐ No, because of other reasons (in school, etc.)

13. **What is the highest degree or level of school that you have completed?** *Mark the one answer that describes the highest grade or degree that you have completed.*
    - ☐ 12 years or less of school (no diploma)
    - ☐ High school graduate—traditional diploma
    - ☐ High school graduate—alternative diploma (home school, GED, etc.)
    - ☐ Some college credit, but less than 1 year
    - ☐ 1 or more years of college, no degree
    - ☐ Associate's degree (e.g., AA, AS)
    - ☐ Bachelor's degree (e.g., BA, AB, BS)
    - ☐ Master's, doctoral, or professional school degree (e.g., MA, MS, MEd, MEng, MBA, MSW, PhD, MD, JD, DVM, EdD)

For the next questions, the definition of "child, children, other legal dependents" includes anyone in your family, except your spouse, who has, or is eligible to have, a Uniformed Services Identification and Privilege card (also called a military ID card) or is eligible for military health care benefits, and is enrolled in the Defense Enrollment Eligibility Reporting System (DEERS).

---

14. **Do you have a child, children, or other legal dependents based on the definition above?**
    - ☐ Yes
    - ☐ No

15. **How many children or other legal dependents do you have in each age group?** *Mark one answer in each row. To indicate none, select "0". To indicate nine or more, select "9".*

a. 5 years and younger   ⬚ ⬚ ⬚ ⬚ ⬚ ⬚ ⬚ ⬚ ⬚ ⬚

b. 6 - 9 years old   ⬚ ⬚ ⬚ ⬚ ⬚ ⬚ ⬚ ⬚ ⬚ ⬚

c. 10 - 22 years old   ⬚ ⬚ ⬚ ⬚ ⬚ ⬚ ⬚ ⬚ ⬚ ⬚

d. 23 years and older   ⬚ ⬚ ⬚ ⬚ ⬚ ⬚ ⬚ ⬚ ⬚ ⬚

16. Are you Spanish/Hispanic/Latino?

- ☐ No, not Spanish/Hispanic/Latino
- ☐ Yes, Mexican, Mexican-American, Chicano, Puerto Rican, Cuban, or other Spanish/Hispanic/Latino

17. What is your race? *Mark one or more races to indicate what race you consider yourself to be.*

- ☐ White
- ☐ Black or African-American
- ☐ American Indian or Alaska Native
- ☐ Asian (e.g., Asian Indian, Chinese, Filipino, Japanese, Korean, Vietnamese)
- ☐ Native Hawaiian or other Pacific Islander (e.g., Samoan, Guamanian or Chamorro)

18. Where is your permanent duty station (homeport) located?

- ☐ In one of the 50 states, D.C., Puerto Rico, or a U.S. territory or possession
- ☐ Europe (e.g., Bosnia-Herzegovina, Germany, Italy, Serbia, United Kingdom)
- ☐ Former Soviet Union (e.g., Russia, Tajikistan, Uzbekistan)
- ☐ East Asia and Pacific (e.g., Australia, Japan, Korea)
- ☐ North Africa, Near East, or South Asia (e.g., Bahrain, Diego Garcia, Kuwait, Saudi Arabia)
- ☐ Sub-Saharan Africa (e.g., Kenya, South Africa)
- ☐ Western Hemisphere (e.g., Cuba, Honduras, Peru)
- ☐ Other or not sure

within one of the 50 states, D.C., Puerto Rico, or a U.S. territory or possession.

Please select ▼

Please specify the name of the country or installation where your permanent duty station (homeport) is located.

19. Where do you live at your permanent duty station?

- ☐ Aboard ship
- ☐ Barracks/dorm/BEQ/UEPH/BOQ/UOPH military facility
- ☐ Military family housing, on base
- ☐ Military family housing, off base
- ☐ Privatized military housing that you rent on base
- ☐ Privatized military housing that you rent off base
- ☐ Civilian/community housing that you own or pay mortgage on
- ☐ Civilian/community housing that you rent
- ☐ Other

Please specify where you live at your permanent duty station.

SATISFACTION

20. **Taking all things into consideration, how satisfied are you, in general, with each of the following aspects of being in the military?**

	Very satisfied	Satisfied	Neither satisfied nor dissatisfied	Dissatisfied	Very dissatisfied
a. Your total compensation (i.e., base pay, allowances, and bonuses)	☐	☐	☐	☐	☐
b. The type of work you do in your military job	☐	☐	☐	☐	☐
c. Your opportunities for promotion	☐	☐	☐	☐	☐
d. The quality of your coworkers	☐	☐	☐	☐	☐
e. The quality of your supervisor	☐	☐	☐	☐	☐

21. Overall, how satisfied are you with the military way of life?
- ☐ Very satisfied
- ☐ Satisfied
- ☐ Neither satisfied nor dissatisfied
- ☐ Dissatisfied
- ☐ Very dissatisfied

22. How many years of active duty service have you completed (including enlisted, warrant officer, and commissioned officer time)? *To indicate less than 1 year, enter "0". To indicate 35 years or more, enter "35".*

☐ Years

23. Suppose that you have to decide whether to stay on active duty. Assuming you could stay, how likely is it that you would choose to do so?
- ☐ Very likely
- ☐ Likely
- ☐ Neither likely nor unlikely
- ☐ Unlikely
- ☐ Very unlikely

24. Does your <u>spouse or significant other</u> think you should stay on or leave active duty?

- ☐ Strongly favors staying
- ☐ Somewhat favors staying
- ☐ Has no opinion one way or the other
- ☐ Somewhat favors leaving
- ☐ Strongly favors leaving

25. Does your <u>family</u> think you should stay on or leave active duty?

- ☐ Strongly favors staying
- ☐ Somewhat favors staying
- ☐ Has no opinion one way or the other
- ☐ Somewhat favors leaving
- ☐ Strongly favors leaving

RETENTION

26. To what extent do you agree or disagree with the following statements?

		Strongly agree	Agree	Neither agree nor disagree	Disagree	Strongly disagree
a.	I enjoy serving in the military.	☐	☐	☐	☐	☐
b.	Serving in the military is consistent with my personal goals.	☐	☐	☐	☐	☐
c.	If I left the military, I would feel like I am starting all over again.	☐	☐	☐	☐	☐
d.	I would feel guilty if I left the military.	☐	☐	☐	☐	☐
e.	Generally, on a day-to-day basis, I am happy with my life in the military.	☐	☐	☐	☐	☐

(Continued) To what extent do you agree or disagree with the following statements?

	Strongly agree	Agree	Neither agree nor disagree	Disagree	Strongly disagree
f. It would be difficult for me to leave the military and give up the benefits that are available in the Service.	☐	☐	☐	☐	☐
g. I would not leave the military right now because I have a sense of obligation to the people in it.	☐	☐	☐	☐	☐
h. I really feel as if the military's values are my own.	☐	☐	☐	☐	☐
i. I would have difficulty finding a job if I left the military.	☐	☐	☐	☐	☐
j. Generally, on a day-to-day basis, I am proud to be in the military.	☐	☐	☐	☐	☐
k. If I left the military, I would feel like I had let my country down.	☐	☐	☐	☐	☐
l. I continue to serve in the military because leaving would require considerable sacrifice.	☐	☐	☐	☐	☐
m. I feel like being a member of the military can help me achieve what I want in life.	☐	☐	☐	☐	☐
n. One of the problems with leaving the military would be the lack of available alternatives.	☐	☐	☐	☐	☐
o. I am committed to making the military my career.	☐	☐	☐	☐	☐

27. When you leave active duty, how likely is it that you will join a National Guard or Reserve unit?

☐ Does not apply, retiring or otherwise ineligible

☐ Very likely

☐ Likely

☐ Neither likely nor unlikely

☐ Unlikely

☐ Very unlikely

TEMPO

28. Have you ever made a Permanent Change of Station (PCS)?

☐ Yes

☐ No

29. How many months has it been since your last PCS? *To indicate less than one month, enter "0". To indicate more than 99 months, enter "99".*

☐ Months

30. In the past 12 months, how many days have you had to work longer than your normal duty day (i.e., overtime)? *To indicate none, enter "0".*

☐ Days

31. In the past 12 months, how many nights have you been away from your permanent duty station (homeport) because of your military duties? *To indicate none, enter "0".*

☐ Nights

32. In the past 24 months, have you been deployed longer than 30 consecutive days?

☐ Yes

☐ No

33. Are you currently on a deployment that has lasted longer than 30 consecutive days?

☐ Yes

☐ No

34. Where are you currently deployed?

- ☐ In one of the 50 states, D.C., Puerto Rico, or a U.S. territory or possession
- ☐ Afghanistan
- ☐ Iraq
- ☐ Other North African, Near Eastern or South Asian country (e.g., Bahrain, Diego Garcia, Kuwait, Saudi Arabia)
- ☐ Europe (e.g., Bosnia-Herzegovina, Germany, Italy, Serbia, United Kingdom)
- ☐ Former Soviet Union (e.g., Russia, Tajikistan, Uzbekistan)
- ☐ East Asia and Pacific (e.g., Australia, Japan, Korea)
- ☐ Sub-Saharan Africa (e.g., Kenya, Liberia, South Africa)
- ☐ Western Hemisphere (e.g., Cuba, Honduras, Peru)
- ☐ Other or not sure

Please select from the list below your deployment location within one of the 50 states, D.C., Puerto Rico, or a U.S. territory or possession.

Please select ▼

Please enter the name of the country or installation where you are currently deployed.

35. In the past 12 months, have you spent more or less time away from your permanent duty station (homeport) than you expected when you first entered the military?

- ☐ Much more than expected
- ☐ More than expected
- ☐ Neither more nor less than expected
- ☐ Less than expected
- ☐ Much less than expected

36. **What impact has time away (or lack thereof) from your permanent duty station (homeport) in the past 12 months had on your military career intentions?**
   - ☐ Greatly increased your desire to stay
   - ☐ Increased your desire to stay
   - ☐ Neither increased nor decreased your desire to stay
   - ☐ Decreased your desire to stay
   - ☐ Greatly decreased your desire to stay

37. **Overall, how well prepared are you to perform your wartime job?**
   - ☐ Very well prepared
   - ☐ Well prepared
   - ☐ Neither well nor poorly prepared
   - ☐ Poorly prepared
   - ☐ Very poorly prepared

38. **Overall, how well prepared is your unit to perform its wartime mission?**
   - ☐ Very well prepared
   - ☐ Well prepared
   - ☐ Neither well nor poorly prepared
   - ☐ Poorly prepared
   - ☐ Very poorly prepared

39. **How well has your training prepared you to perform your wartime job?**
   - ☐ Very well
   - ☐ Well
   - ☐ Neither well nor poorly
   - ☐ Poorly
   - ☐ Very poorly

40. How well has your training prepared you to perform your wartime job in support of joint operations?

- ☐ Very well
- ☐ Well
- ☐ Neither well nor poorly
- ☐ Poorly
- ☐ Very poorly

STRESS

41. Overall, how would you rate the current level of stress in your <u>work</u> life?

- ☐ Much less than usual
- ☐ Less than usual
- ☐ About the same as usual
- ☐ More than usual
- ☐ Much more than usual

42. Overall, how would you rate the current level of stress in your <u>personal</u> life?

- ☐ Much less than usual
- ☐ Less than usual
- ☐ About the same as usual
- ☐ More than usual
- ☐ Much more than usual

43. **In the past month, how often have you...**

	Never	Almost never	Sometimes	Fairly often	Very often
a. Felt nervous and stressed?	☐	☐	☐	☐	☐
b. Felt that you were unable to control the important things in your life?	☐	☐	☐	☐	☐
c. Been upset because of something that happened unexpectedly?	☐	☐	☐	☐	
d. Been angered because of things that were outside of your control?	☐	☐	☐	☐	☐
e. Felt difficulties were piling up so high that you could not overcome them?	☐	☐	☐	☐	
f. Found that you could not cope with all of the things you had to do?	☐	☐	☐	☐	☐

DEPLOYMENTS SINCE SEPTEMBER 11, 2001

44. **Since September 11, 2001, how many times have you been deployed for any of the following operations?** *Mark one answer in each row. To indicate none, select "0 times".*

	0 times	1 time	2 times	3 or more times
a. Operation Noble Eagle (airport security)	☐	☐	☐	☐
b. Operation Enduring Freedom (Afghanistan)	☐	☐	☐	☐
c. Operation Iraqi Freedom	☐	☐	☐	☐
d. Other	☐	☐	☐	☐

Please specify the other operation for which you were deployed since September 11, 2001.

☐

45. Since September 11, 2001, how many times have you been deployed?

46. Since September 11, 2001, what is the total number of days you have been away from your permanent duty station (homeport)?

47. Since September 11, 2001, have you been deployed to a combat zone or an area where you drew imminent danger pay or hostile fire pay?
☐ Yes
☐ No

48. Since September 11, 2001, how many days have you been deployed to a combat zone?

49. <u>For your most recent deployment</u>, how many months have you been or were you deployed to an area where you drew imminent danger pay or hostile fire pay? *<u>Include</u> partial months. For example, even if you were deployed to a combat zone for 2 days, and those days were in different months, enter "2".*

50. Were you involved in combat operations?
☐ Yes
☐ No

50. Were you involved in combat operations?
☐ Yes
☐ No

51. Are you currently deployed to a combat zone or an area where you are drawing imminent danger pay or hostile fire pay?
☐ Yes
☐ No

52. Were any of your deployments since September 11, 2001 longer than you expected?
☐ Yes
☐ No

53. Since September 11, 2001, have you been under stop-loss at any time?

- ☐ Yes
- ☐ No

MILITARY ONESOURCE

54. In the <u>past 12 months</u>, have you used the confidential Military OneSource in the following ways to obtain information or services? *Mark "Yes" or "No" for each item.*

	Yes	No
a. Accessed www.MilitaryOneSource.com	☐	☐
b. E-mailed Military OneSource	☐	☐
c. Talked on the telephone with a Military OneSource consultant (1-800-342-9647)	☐	☐
d. Used Military OneSource to arrange face-to-face counseling session(s)	☐	☐

55. How useful was Military OneSource.com?

- ☐ Very useful
- ☐ Useful
- ☐ Somewhat useful
- ☐ Not useful

56. How useful was e-mail communication with a Military OneSource consultant?

- ☐ Very useful
- ☐ Useful
- ☐ Somewhat useful
- ☐ Not useful

57. How useful was the Military OneSource confidential telephonic counseling?

- ☐ Very useful
- ☐ Useful
- ☐ Somewhat useful
- ☐ Not useful

58. How useful were the Military OneSource in-person counseling referrals?

- ☐ Very useful
- ☐ Useful
- ☐ Somewhat useful
- ☐ Not useful

59. Please rate Military OneSource (1-800-342-9647) on the following issues. *If you have not used the feature, please select "Not applicable". Mark one for each row.*

	Very useful	Useful	Somewhat useful	Not useful	Not applicable
a. Personal and relationship issues	☐	☐	☐	☐	☐
b. Child care and parenting issues	☐	☐	☐	☐	☐
c. Deployment and reunion issues	☐	☐	☐	☐	☐
d. Education for children (K-12, college, and special needs)	☐	☐	☐	☐	☐
e. Spouse training, education, and career	☐	☐	☐	☐	☐
f. Elder care issues	☐	☐	☐	☐	☐
g. Money matters	☐	☐	☐	☐	☐
h. Legal issues	☐	☐	☐	☐	☐
i. Relocation	☐	☐	☐	☐	☐
j. Transition to civilian life	☐	☐	☐	☐	☐
k. Healthy habits	☐	☐	☐	☐	☐
l. Translation assistance	☐	☐	☐	☐	☐

60. In the past 12 months, have you and/or your spouse used Military OneSource for financial counseling?

- ☐ Yes
- ☐ No

IMPACT OF DEPLOYMENTS

61. While you were away during your most recent deployment, to what extent were the following a concern?

	Very large extent	Large extent	Moderate extent	Small extent	Not a concern
a. Spouse's job or education demands	☐	☐	☐	☐	☐
b. Managing bills and expenses	☐	☐	☐	☐	☐
c. Household repairs, yard work, or car maintenance	☐	☐	☐	☐	☐
d. Loss of income from part-time job	☐	☐	☐	☐	☐
e. Safety of your family in their community	☐	☐	☐	☐	☐
f. Your feelings of anxiety or depression	☐	☐	☐	☐	☐
g. Serious health problems in the family	☐	☐	☐	☐	☐
h. Serious emotional problems in the family	☐	☐	☐	☐	☐
i. Technical difficulties communicating with spouse/family	☐	☐	☐	☐	☐
j. Difficulty maintaining emotional connection with spouse/family	☐	☐	☐	☐	☐
k. Major financial hardship or bankruptcy	☐	☐	☐	☐	☐
l. Birth or adoption of a child	☐	☐	☐	☐	☐
m. Marital problems	☐	☐	☐	☐	☐
n. Your feelings of loneliness	☐	☐	☐	☐	☐
o. Managing child care/child schedules	☐	☐	☐	☐	☐
p. Increased need for child care	☐	☐	☐	☐	☐
q. Had to find child care that was not previously needed	☐	☐	☐	☐	☐
r. Your difficulty sleeping	☐	☐	☐	☐	☐

(Continued) <u>While you were away during your most recent deployment, to what extent were the following a concern?</u>

	Very large extent	Large extent	Moderate extent	Small extent	Not a concern
s. Unintended weight gain or loss	☐	☐	☐	☐	☐
t. Your ability to continue your college education	☐	☐	☐	☐	☐
u. Other	☐	☐	☐	☐	☐

62. **After your most recent deployment, to what extent were you likely to . . . ?** *Mark one answer in each row.*

	Very large extent	Large extent	Moderate extent	Small extent	Not at all
a. Be more emotionally distant (e.g., less talkative, less affectionate, less interested in social life)	☐	☐	☐	☐	☐
b. Appreciate life more	☐	☐	☐	☐	☐
c. Get angry faster	☐	☐	☐	☐	☐
d. Appreciate your family and friends more	☐	☐	☐	☐	☐
e. Drink more alcohol	☐	☐	☐	☐	☐
f. Have more confidence in yourself	☐	☐	☐	☐	☐
g. Take more risks with your safety	☐	☐	☐	☐	☐
h. Be different in another way	☐	☐	☐	☐	☐

How were you different after your most recent deployment?

63. Did you receive support services (e.g., support groups, counseling) after returning home from your most recent deployment?

   ☐ Yes, and it helped

   ☐ Yes, but it did not help

   ☐ No, I did not want support services

   ☐ No, but I wanted support services

   ☐ Don't know

64. Have you had reunion and reintegration support from any of the following sources? *Mark "Yes" or "No" for each item.*

	Yes	No
a. Family Readiness/Support Group	☐	☐
b. Military OneSource	☐	☐
c. Faith based organization (e.g., church, synagogue, mosque)	☐	☐
d. Services in your civilian community	☐	☐
e. Other military-sponsored program	☐	☐
f. Other program	☐	☐

65. **In response to being deployed, did you talk to anyone about...** *Mark one answer for each item.*

	Yes, and it helped me	Yes, but it did not help me	No, and I did not want to talk to anyone about this topic	No, but I wanted to talk to someone about this topic
a. Problem solving?	☐	☐	☐	☐
b. Coping with stress?	☐	☐	☐	☐
c. Financial management?	☐	☐	☐	☐
d. Family issues?	☐	☐	☐	☐
e. Marital issues?	☐	☐	☐	☐
f. Dealing with family separations?	☐	☐	☐	☐
g. Parent/child communication?	☐	☐	☐	☐
h. Deployment and reunion?	☐	☐	☐	☐
i. Crisis situations?	☐	☐	☐	☐
j. Grief and loss?	☐	☐	☐	☐

66. **Which of the following describes your readjustment to being back at home after your most recent deployment?**

☐ Very easy

☐ Easy

☐ Neither easy nor difficult

☐ Difficult

☐ Very difficult

67. **In response to your most recent deployment, did <u>your child(ren)</u> experience any of the following behavioral changes?** *Mark one answer in each row. Where your child(ren)'s behavior did not change, please mark "No change".*

	Increased	No change	Decreased	Don't know
a. Academic performance	☐	☐	☐	
b. Problem behavior at school	☐	☐	☐	☐
c. Problem behavior at home	☐	☐	☐	
d. Pride in having a military parent	☐	☐	☐	☐
e. Fear/anxiety	☐	☐	☐	
f. Independence	☐	☐	☐	☐
g. Being responsible	☐	☐	☐	
h. Closeness to family members	☐	☐	☐	☐
i. Closeness to friends	☐	☐	☐	☐
j. Distress over discussions of the war in the home, school, or media	☐	☐	☐	☐
k. Anger about my military requirements	☐	☐	☐	☐
l. Other behavior(s)	☐	☐	☐	☐

Please specify what other behavioral change(s) your child(ren) experienced in response to your most recent deployment.

68. How important are the following in your child(ren)'s ability to cope with your deployments? *Mark one answer in each row.*

	Very important	Important	Moderately important	Somewhat important	Not important
a. Communications with the deployed parent	☐	☐	☐	☐	☐
b. Spouse/guardian support for the deployment	☐	☐	☐	☐	☐
c. Spouse/guardian ability to maintain a stable household routine	☐	☐	☐	☐	☐
d. Caregiver/teacher reaction to deployment	☐	☐	☐	☐	☐
e. The way family members deal with the deployment	☐	☐	☐	☐	☐
f. Geographic stability during deployment (i.e., no relocations, changes in schools)	☐	☐	☐	☐	☐
g. Limited exposure to media coverage of the war	☐	☐	☐	☐	☐
h. Other	☐	☐	☐	☐	☐

Please specify other important factors that help your child(ren) cope with deployments.

TOBACCO

69. **To what extent does your supervisor allow more breaks for tobacco users than non-tobacco users?**
   - ☐ Very large extent
   - ☐ Large extent
   - ☐ Moderate extent
   - ☐ Small extent
   - ☐ Not at all

70. **Have you used any tobacco products (cigarettes, pipe, cigars, smokeless tobacco) within the last 12 months?**
   - ☐ Yes
   - ☐ No

71. **How would you classify yourself as a tobacco user?**
   - ☐ Current user of tobacco products
   - ☐ Quit within the past 6 months
   - ☐ Quit more than 6 months ago
   - ☐ Occasional user of tobacco products

72. **Did you take any steps in the past six months to quit using tobacco products?**
   - ☐ Yes
   - ☐ No

73. **Are you seriously considering quitting use of tobacco products?**
   - ☐ Yes, within the next six months
   - ☐ Yes, but not within the next six months
   - ☐ Yes, but not sure when
   - ☐ No

74. **Have you identified an action plan to quit using tobacco in the next month?**
   - ☐ Yes
   - ☐ No

75. **Have you heard, read, or seen messages or advertising <u>on base</u> in the past month that would encourage you to quit using tobacco?**

    ☐ Yes

    ☐ No

    ☐

76. **Did any of the messages have the tagline "Make Everyone Proud?"**

    ☐ Yes

    ☐ No

77. **Where did you hear or see the "Make Everyone Proud" advertisement?** *Mark "Yes" or "No" for each item.*

	Yes	No
a. Radio	☐	☐
b. Base newspaper	☐	☐
c. Poster	☐	☐
d. Other	☐	☐

Please specify where you saw or heard the "Make Everyone Proud" advertisement.

☐

78. **Please specify what you recall about the "Make Everyone Proud" advertisement.**

☐

79. **Did you take any of the following actions as a result of hearing the "Make Everyone Proud" advertisement?** *Mark "Yes" or "No" for each item.*

	Yes	No
a. Made the decision to quit using tobacco	☐	☐
b. Began/resumed thinking about quitting use of tobacco products	☐	☐
c. Visited the Web site noted in the advertisement	☐	☐
d. Initiated other action toward quitting use of tobacco (e.g., spoke to health professional, bought patches, threw out tobacco products)	☐	☐
e. Actually quit using tobacco	☐	☐
f. Other action	☐	☐

LEADERSHIP

80. **To what extent do you agree or disagree with each of the following statements about your supervisor?**

	Strongly agree	Agree	Neither agree nor disagree	Disagree	Strongly disagree
a. You trust your supervisor	☐	☐	☐	☐	☐
b. Your supervisor ensures that all assigned people are treated fairly	☐	☐	☐	☐	☐
c. There is conflict between your supervisor and the people who report to him/her	☐	☐	☐	☐	☐
d. You are satisfied with the direction/supervision you receive from your supervisor	☐	☐	☐	☐	☐
e. Your supervisor evaluates work performance fairly	☐	☐	☐	☐	☐
f. Your supervisor makes work assignments fairly in your workplace	☐	☐	☐	☐	☐

81. Overall, how satisfied are you with <u>leadership</u> in your unit?

- ☐ Very satisfied
- ☐ Satisfied
- ☐ Neither satisfied nor dissatisfied
- ☐ Dissatisfied
- ☐ Very dissatisfied

82. Overall, how satisfied are you with <u>management</u> in your unit?

- ☐ Very satisfied
- ☐ Satisfied
- ☐ Neither satisfied nor dissatisfied
- ☐ Dissatisfied
- ☐ Very dissatisfied

83. Overall, how good a job do you feel is being done by your immediate supervisor?

- ☐ Very good
- ☐ Good
- ☐ Fair
- ☐ Poor
- ☐ Very poor

ORGANIZATIONAL EFFECTIVENESS

84. **To what extent do you agree or disagree with the following statements about the people with whom you work?**

	Strongly agree	Agree	Neither agree nor disagree	Disagree	Strongly disagree
a. There is very little conflict among your coworkers.	☐	☐	☐	☐	☐
b. You like your coworkers.	☐	☐	☐	☐	☐
c. Your coworkers put forth the effort required for their jobs.	☐	☐	☐	☐	☐
d. You are satisfied with the relationships you have with your coworkers.	☐	☐	☐	☐	☐
e. The people in your workgroup tend to get along.	☐	☐	☐	☐	☐
f. The people in your workgroup are willing to help each other.	☐	☐	☐	☐	☐

85. **To what extent do you agree or disagree with the following statements about the work you do?**

	Strongly agree	Agree	Neither agree nor disagree	Disagree	Strongly disagree
a. Your work provides you with a sense of pride.	☐	☐	☐	☐	☐
b. Your work makes good use of your skills.	☐	☐	☐	☐	☐
c. Your present assignment is good for your military career.	☐	☐	☐	☐	☐
d. You like the kind of work you do.	☐	☐	☐	☐	☐
e. Your job gives you the chance to acquire valuable skills.	☐	☐	☐	☐	☐
f. You are satisfied with your job as a whole.	☐	☐	☐	☐	☐

86. **To what extent do you agree or disagree with the following statements about the** *effectiveness of your workgroup* **(all persons who report to the same supervisor that you do)?**

	Strongly agree	Agree	Neither agree nor disagree	Disagree	Strongly disagree
a. The amount of output of my workgroup is very high.	☐	☐	☐	☐	☐
b. The quality of output of my workgroup is very high.	☐	☐	☐	☐	☐
c. When high-priority work arises, such as short suspenses, crash programs, and schedule changes, the people in my workgroup do an outstanding job in handling these situations.	☐	☐	☐	☐	☐
d. My workgroup always gets maximum output from available resources (e.g., personnel and materials).	☐	☐	☐	☐	☐
e. My workgroup's performance in comparison to similar workgroups is very high.	☐	☐	☐	☐	☐

MENTORING

87. <u>In your opinion</u>, **have you ever had a mentor?**

- ☐ Yes, you have one now
- ☐ Yes, you had one, but you don't have one now
- ☐ No, but you would have liked one
- ☐ No, and you never wanted one
- ☐ No, and you don't know what a mentor is

88. Is your current mentor (or was your <u>most recent</u> mentor) . . . ? *Mark one.*

☐ Your rater

☐ Your senior rater

☐ A person who is/was higher in rank than you, but not your rater or your senior rater

☐ A person who is/was at your same rank

☐ A person who is/was lower in rank than you

☐ A person who is not or was not in the military at the time the mentoring was provided

89. If your current mentor (or if none now, your <u>most recent</u> mentor) provides the following assistance, how helpful is/was each to you?

	Extremely helpful	Very helpful	Moderately helpful	Slightly helpful	Not at all helpful	Not provided
a. Teaches job skills	☐	☐	☐	☐	☐	☐
b. Gives feedback on your job performance	☐	☐	☐	☐	☐	☐
c. Assigns challenging tasks	☐	☐	☐	☐	☐	☐
d. Helps develop your skills/competencies for future assignments	☐	☐	☐	☐	☐	☐
e. Provides support and encouragement	☐	☐	☐	☐	☐	☐
f. Provides personal and social guidance	☐	☐	☐	☐	☐	☐
g. Provides career guidance	☐	☐	☐	☐	☐	☐
h. Demonstrates trust	☐	☐	☐	☐	☐	☐
i. Acts as a role model	☐	☐	☐	☐	☐	☐
j. Protects you	☐	☐	☐	☐	☐	☐
k. Invites you to observe activities at his/her level	☐	☐	☐	☐	☐	☐
l. Instills Service core values	☐	☐	☐	☐	☐	☐
m. Provides moral/ethical guidance	☐	☐	☐	☐	☐	☐
n. Teaches/advises on organizational politics	☐	☐	☐	☐	☐	☐

(Continued) If your current mentor (or if none now, your <u>most recent</u> mentor) provides the following assistance, how helpful is/was each to you?

	Extremely helpful	Very helpful	Moderately helpful	Slightly helpful	Not at all helpful	Not provided
o. Provides sponsorship/contacts to advance your career	☐	☐	☐	☐	☐	☐
p. Assists in obtaining future assignments	☐	☐	☐	☐	☐	☐

ORGANIZATIONAL CULTURE

90. Indicate the extent to which you agree or disagree with the following statements about your unit/Service?

	Strongly agree	Agree	Neither agree nor disagree	Disagree	Strongly disagree
a. The current environment in your **unit** is one of "zero" defect (i.e., a feeling that one mistake will end a career)	☐	☐	☐	☐	☐
b. The current environment in your **Service** is one of "zero defect"	☐	☐	☐	☐	☐
c. Micromanagement is prevalent in your **unit**	☐	☐	☐	☐	☐
d. Micromanagement is prevalent in your **Service**	☐	☐	☐	☐	☐

91. Please indicate whether you agree or disagree with the following statements?

	Strongly agree	Agree	Neither agree nor disagree	Disagree	Strongly disagree
a. If you make a request through channels in your unit, you know somebody will listen	☐	☐	☐	☐	☐
b. Leaders in your unit are more interested in looking good than in being good	☐	☐	☐	☐	☐
c. You would go for help with a personal problem to people in your chain-of-command	☐	☐	☐	☐	☐
d. Leaders in your unit are not concerned with the way the Service members treat each other as long as the job gets done	☐	☐	☐	☐	☐
e. You are impressed with the quality of leadership in your unit	☐	☐	☐	☐	☐
f. Leaders in your unit are more interested in furthering their careers than in the well-being of their Service members	☐	☐	☐	☐	☐

CAREER OPPORTUNITIES

92. When you first entered active duty service, did you have a preference for a military occupation?

☐ Yes

☐ No

93. Did you receive the military occupation of your choice?

☐ Yes

☐ No, but I received a related occupation

☐ No, I received an occupation unrelated to my choice

94. How satisfied are you now with the military occupation you received when you first entered active duty?

☐ Very satisfied

☐ Satisfied

☐ Neither satisfied nor dissatisfied

☐ Dissatisfied

☐ Very dissatisfied

95. How much do you agree with the following statements about your military career and Service?

	Strongly agree	Agree	Neither agree nor disagree	Disagree	Strongly disagree
a. I will get the assignments I need to be competitive for promotions	☐	☐	☐	☐	☐
b. My Service's evaluation/selection system is effective in promoting its best members	☐	☐	☐	☐	☐
c. If I stay in the Service, I will be promoted as high as my ability and effort warrant	☐	☐	☐	☐	☐

96. How satisfied are you with the following aspects of your career?

	Very satisfied	Satisfied	Neither satisfied nor dissatisfied	Dissatisfied	Very dissatisfied
a. Your level of responsibility on the job	☐	☐	☐	☐	☐
b. Your level of authority on the job	☐	☐	☐	☐	☐
c. Your opportunities for promotion	☐	☐	☐	☐	☐
d. Your chances to acquire valuable job skills	☐	☐	☐	☐	☐

97. If you stay on active duty, when would you expect your next promotion to a higher grade?

- ☐ Less than 3 months
- ☐ 3 months to less than 7 months
- ☐ 7 months to less than 1 year
- ☐ 1 year to less than 2 years
- ☐ 2 years or more
- ☐ Does not apply, I do not expect a promotion
- ☐ Does not apply, I have no opportunities for promotion

98. Have you completed a professional development course (for example, Basic Non-Commissioned Officers Course [BNCO], Command and General Staff College)? *Mark only one answer.*

- ☐ Yes, via correspondence
- ☐ Yes, in-residence
- ☐ Yes, both via correspondence and in-residence
- ☐ No

99. How many professional development courses have you completed?

- ☐ One
- ☐ Two
- ☐ Three or more

100. To what extent did completing a professional development course enhance your performance as a Soldier/Sailor/Marine/Airman?

- ☐ Very large extent
- ☐ Large extent
- ☐ Moderate extent
- ☐ Small extent
- ☐ Not at all

101. To what extent did completing a professional development course enhance your chance of being promoted?

- ☐ Very large extent
- ☐ Large extent
- ☐ Moderate extent
- ☐ Small extent
- ☐ Not at all

102. Which form of professional development, correspondence or in-residence, was more beneficial in terms of your development as a Soldier/Sailor/Marine/Airman?

- ☐ Correspondence was much more beneficial
- ☐ Correspondence was more beneficial
- ☐ Correspondence and in-residence were equally beneficial
- ☐ In-residence was more beneficial
- ☐ In-residence was much more beneficial

103. Which form of professional development, correspondence or in-residence, was more beneficial in terms of your enhancing your chances of being promoted?

- ☐ Correspondence was much more beneficial
- ☐ Correspondence was more beneficial
- ☐ Correspondence and in-residence were equally beneficial
- ☐ In-residence was more beneficial
- ☐ In-residence was much more beneficial

104. **Assuming you were going to PCS in the next 12 months, how desirable would each of the following assignments be to you in terms of quality of life?**

		Highly		Neither desirable nor		Highly
a.	Unaccompanied tour to Korea (24 months)	☐	☐	☐	☐	☐
b.	Unaccompanied tour to Korea (12 months)	☐	☐	☐	☐	☐
c.	Accompanied tour to Korea (36 months)	☐	☐	☐	☐	☐
d.	Accompanied tour to Korea (24 months)	☐	☐	☐	☐	☐
e.	Unaccompanied tour to Guam (24 months)	☐	☐			
f.	Accompanied tour to Guam (36 months)	☐	☐	☐	☐	☐
g.	Unaccompanied tour to Japan (24 months)	☐	☐			
h.	Accompanied tour to Japan (36 months)	☐	☐	☐	☐	☐
i.	Unaccompanied tour to Germany (24 months)	☐	☐			
j.	Accompanied tour to Germany (36 months)	☐	☐	☐	☐	☐
k.	Unaccompanied tour to Bahrain (12 months)	☐	☐			
l.	Accompanied tour to Bahrain (24 months)	☐	☐	☐	☐	☐
m.	Unaccompanied tour to Saudi Arabia (12 months)	☐	☐	☐	☐	☐
n.	Accompanied tour to Saudi Arabia (24 months)	☐	☐	☐	☐	☐
o.	Unaccompanied tour to to Kuwait	☐	☐	☐	☐	☐

81

| p. | Accompanied tour to Kuwait (24 months) | ☐ | ☐ | ☐ | ☐ | ☐ |

(Continued) Assuming you were going to PCS in the next 12 months, how desirable would each of the following assignments be to you in terms of quality of life?

		Highly desirable	Desirable	Neither desirable nor undesirable	Undesirable	Highly undesirable
q.	Unaccompanied tour to Cuba (12 months)	☐	☐	☐	☐	☐
r.	Accompanied tour to Cuba (24 months)	☐	☐	☐	☐	☐
s.	Unaccompanied tour to Turkey (15 months)	☐	☐	☐	☐	☐
t.	Accompanied tour to Turkey (24 months)	☐	☐	☐	☐	☐

TAKING THE SURVEY

105. Where did you take this survey? *Mark "Yes" or "No" for each item.*

		Yes	No
a.	Deployed location (on land)	☐	☐
b.	On ship at sea	☐	☐
c.	On board a ship in port	☐	
d.	TDY or training location	☐	☐
e.	Non-military location (e.g., public library, Wi-Fi hotspot)	☐	☐
f.	Home/barracks	☐	☐
g.	Work/office	☐	
h.	Installation/ship library	☐	☐
i.	Installation/ship recreation center	☐	☐
j.	Other location on installation	☐	☐

Please specify where you took this survey.

```
┌──────────────────────────────────────────────┬─┐
│                                              │▲│
│                                              │ │
│                                              │ │
│                                              │ │
│                                              │▼│
└──────────────────────────────────────────────┴─┘
```

106. **Which of the following computers did you use to take the survey?** *Mark "Yes" or "No" for each item.*

	Yes	No
a. Government computer		
b. Privately owned computer	☐	☐
c. Public (e.g., library or cafe) computer	☐	☐
d. Other	☐	☐

107. **If you have comments or concerns that you were not able to express in answering this survey, please enter them in the space provided. Your feedback is useful and appreciated.**

```
┌──────────────────────────────────────────────┬─┐
│                                              │▲│
│                                              │ │
│                                              │ │
│                                              │ │
│                                              │▼│
└──────────────────────────────────────────────┴─┘
```

84

Appendix B: Tables B1 through B11

Table B1: (MENTR) Descriptive Statistics

In your opinion, have you ever had a mentor?

		Frequency	Percent	Valid Percent	Cumulative Percent
Valid	Yes, you have one now	791	31.8	31.8	31.8
	Yes, you had one, but you don't have one now	954	38.4	38.4	70.2
	No, but you would have liked one	486	19.5	19.5	89.7
	No, and you never wanted one	239	9.6	9.6	99.3
	No, and you don't know what a mentor is	17	.7	.7	100.0
	Total	2487	100.0	100.0	

Table B2: (XSEXR) Descriptive Statistics

Imputed Gender

		Frequency	Percent	Valid Percent	Cumulative Percent
Valid	Male	1937	77.9	77.9	77.9
	Female	550	22.1	22.1	100.0
	Total	2487	100.0	100.0	

Table B3: (XRETH4R) Descriptive Statistics

Race/Ethnicity - 2 level

		Frequency	Percent	Valid Percent	Cumulative Percent
Valid	White	1765	71.0	71.0	71.0
	Total minority	722	29.0	29.0	100.0
	Total	2487	100.0	100.0	

Table B4: (XMARSTR) Descriptive Statistics

Marital Status

		Frequency	Percent	Valid Percent	Cumulative Percent
Valid	Not married	837	33.7	33.7	33.7
	Married	1650	66.3	66.3	100.0
	Total	2487	100.0	100.0	

Table B5: (YOSCR2) Descriptive Statistics

Recode Years active-duty service

		Frequency	Percent	Valid Percent	Cumulative Percent
Valid	Less than 3 years	382	15.4	15.4	15.4
	3 years to less than 6 years	424	17.0	17.0	32.4
	6 years to less than 10 years	430	17.3	17.3	49.7
	10 or more years	1251	50.3	50.3	100.0
	Total	2487	100.0	100.0	

Table B6: (XPAYGRP2R) Descriptive Statistics

XPAYGRP2R: Pay-grade Group 2 - 5 levels

		Frequency	Percent	Valid Percent	Cumulative Percent
Valid	E1-E4	545	21.9	21.9	21.9
	E5-E9	1118	45.0	45.0	66.9
	O1-O3	403	16.2	16.2	83.1
	O4-O6	421	16.9	16.9	100.0
	Total	2487	100.0	100.0	

Table B7: Job Satisfaction Case Processing Summary, Reliability Statistics, and Scale Statistics

Case Processing Summary

		N	%
Cases	Valid	2408	96.8
	Excluded[a]	79	3.2
	Total	2487	100.0

a. Listwise deletion based on all variables in the procedure.

Reliability Statistics

Cronbach's Alpha	N of Items
.753	6

Scale Statistics

Mean	Variance	Std. Deviation	N of Items
22.48	15.751	3.969	6

Table B8: Retention Case Processing Summary, Reliability Statistics, and Scale Statistics

Case Processing Summary

		N	%
Cases	Valid	2017	81.1
	Excluded[a]	470	18.9
	Total	2487	100.0

a. Listwise deletion based on all variables in the procedure.

Reliability Statistics

Cronbach's Alpha	N of Items
.826	3

Scale Statistics

Mean	Variance	Std. Deviation	N of Items
10.85	10.821	3.290	3

Table B9: Organizational Commitment Case Processing Summary, Reliability Statistics, and Scale Statistics

Case Processing Summary

		N	%
Cases	Valid	2369	95.3
	Excluded[a]	118	4.7
	Total	2487	100.0

a. Listwise deletion based on all variables in the procedure.

Reliability Statistics

Cronbach's Alpha	N of Items
.876	15

Scale Statistics

Mean	Variance	Std. Deviation	N of Items
49.81	91.266	9.553	15

Table B10: Stress Case Processing Summary, Reliability Statistics, and Scale Statistics

Case Processing Summary

		N	%
Cases	Valid	2422	97.4
	Excluded[a]	65	2.6
	Total	2487	100.0

a. Listwise deletion based on all variables in the procedure.

Reliability Statistics

Cronbach's Alpha	N of Items
.886	8

Scale Statistics

Mean	Variance	Std. Deviation	N of Items
27.6003	36.754	6.06250	8

Table B11: T-Test Group Statistics

T-Test Group Statistics

	MENTR_Yes		N	Mean	Std. Deviation	Std. Error Mean
Job_Satisfaction	dimensi	1.00	1692	3.8059	.64725	.01574
	on1	.00	716	3.6043	.67344	.02517
Retention	dimensi	1.00	1449	3.6901	1.08998	.02863
	on1	.00	568	3.4319	1.09228	.04583
Org_Commitment	dimensi	1.00	1665	3.3588	.63464	.01555
	on1	.00	704	3.2313	.63364	.02388
Stress	dimensi	1.00	1698	3.4665	.75847	.01841
	on1	.00	724	3.4114	.75539	.02807

Table B12: T-Test Independent Samples Test

T-Test Independent Samples Test

		Levene's Test for Equality of Variances		t-test for Equality of Means					95% Confidence Interval of the Difference	
		F	Sig.	t	df	Sig. (2-tailed)	Mean Difference	Std. Error Difference	Lower	Upper
Job Satisfaction	Equal variances assumed	2.843	.092	6.901	2406	.000	.20157	.02921	.14429	.25884
	Equal variances not assumed			6.791	1299.285	.000	.20157	.02968	.14334	.25980
Retention	Equal variances assumed	.006	.939	4.782	2015	.000	.25821	.05399	.15232	.36409
	Equal variances not assumed			4.778	1034.331	.000	.25821	.05404	.15216	.36425
Org_ Commitment	Equal variances assumed	.075	.785	4.474	2367	.000	.12759	.02852	.07167	.18351
	Equal variances not assumed			4.477	1325.127	.000	.12759	.02850	.07168	.18350
Stress	Equal variances assumed	.021	.884	1.638	2420	.102	.05508	.03362	-.01086	.12101
	Equal variances not assumed			1.641	1370.302	.101	.05508	.03357	-.01078	.12093